STRATEGIC

CONVERSATIONS

Published by SuccessBooks®, Lake Mary, FL.

SuccessBooks® is a registered trademark.

ISBN: 979-8-9918645-2-7
LCCN: 2024926944

Most SuccessBooks® titles are available at special quantity discounts for bulk purchases for sales promotions, premiums, fundraising, and educational use. Special versions or book excerpts can also be created to fit specific needs.

For more information, please write:

SuccessBooks®
3415 W. Lake Mary Blvd. #950370
Lake Mary, FL 32795
or call 1.877.261.4930

Visit us online at: www.CelebrityPressPublishing.com.

STRATEGIC
CONVERSATIONS

WINNING COMMUNICATION STRATEGIES FOR
LIFE'S MOST IMPORTANT INTERACTIONS

SUCCESS
BOOKS®
Lake Mary, FL

STRATEGIC

CONVERSATIONS

WINNING COMMUNICATION STRATEGIES FOR LIFE'S MOST IMPORTANT INTERACTIONS

SUCCESS
BOOKS®
Lake Mary, FL

CONTENTS

CHAPTER 1

THE ART OF STRATEGIC CONVERSATIONS USING TRUST-BASED INFLUENCE

By Chris Voss

L ife and business thrive—or falter—on the foundation of communication. In every relationship, transaction, or negotiation, what you say and how you say it plays a pivotal role.

Effective communication isn't just about words; it's about creating an environment of trust-based influence, the most long-lasting and durable form of influence.

Navigating any strategic conversation requires preparation and adaptability. When stakes are high, these conversations can mean the difference between success and failure, growth or stagnation. The Black Swan Group's methods aim to master this very art.

Strategic conversations thrive on the ability to uncover the hidden dynamics that influence outcomes. This is where the Black Swan Method comes into play. These skills, which are central to the negotiation and communication philosophy of The Black Swan Group, provide a framework for navigating even the most challenging dialogues. They center on identifying and addressing the unknown or hidden elements—the Black Swans—that can dramatically alter the trajectory of any interaction.

In strategic conversations, Black Swan Skills empower communicators to go beyond the surface, discovering unspoken needs, fears, and motivations. By mastering these skills, you can transform conversations from transactional to transformative, yielding better outcomes while fostering deeper trust and collaboration.

BUILDING TRUST THROUGH COMMUNICATION

At the heart of every effective interaction is trust. Without it no strategy, no carefully chosen words, no dazzling delivery can lead to meaningful outcomes. Trust is most effectively built not by declarations but by expressing your understanding of their perspective—what The Black Swan Group calls *Tactical Empathy.*

This is the ability to see another's perspective and express it out loud to simply make them *feel* heard. When people feel heard, the foundation of trust is laid in a very powerful way. They can't help but feel bonded to you somehow. The extremely counterintuitive aspect of this is you don't need to agree with them or even "like" them for this to take hold. It's like a magic wand.

Imagine a business deal where a CEO is trying to close a critical partnership. The temptation might be to focus on the merits of their proposal. But what if, instead, the CEO starts by addressing the potential partner's concerns?

"You're probably wondering how this will fit into your existing operations."

This opening disarms. It communicates, "I see you. I know what you're thinking." By addressing the fear or skepticism first, you lower defenses, creating a foundation for trust.

The principle applies equally in personal relationships. Imagine a moment of tension with a loved one. Instead of reacting defensively, lead with acknowledgment: "It's clear you're frustrated because I missed the deadline we set."

This statement does more than just state the obvious—it validates their feelings. It shows you care enough to listen and understand, setting the stage for resolution. Tactical empathy is not just a strategy but a commitment to treating people as partners rather than adversaries.

INFLUENCING OUTCOMES THROUGH STRATEGIC CONVERSATIONS

In high-stakes negotiation, the goal is not to impose your will but to lead the conversation in a way that influences decisions and creates the best outcomes. Influence is not about domination. The most effective communicators balance assertiveness with empathy, creating an environment where the other party feels empowered, even as they align with your desired outcome.

In my book *Never Split the Difference*, the concept of the "illusion of control" plays a pivotal role. This strategy involves asking calibrated questions—open-ended queries designed to make the other party think and respond. These questions shift the conversation's power dynamics, placing the ball in their court while subtly guiding the direction of the discussion.

For example, in a hiring negotiation, rather than bluntly stating, "We need you to lower your salary expectations," you might ask, "How do we ensure your salary fits within our budget constraints while still meeting your needs and building your career?"

The shift is subtle but powerful. This turns a demand into a collaborative problem-solving exercise based on shared future success. The other party feels involved and invested in the solution, not just making it easier to reach an agreement, but ensuring collaboration moving forward.

Here's another example: When negotiating a partnership deal with a vendor, instead of arguing about numbers or meeting "halfway" (always a poor idea), ask, "What would need to happen for you to feel comfortable adjusting the terms?"

That question reframes the situation. It changes the tone from confrontation to collaboration. The vendor will feel engaged in the solution and ultimately will come to trust you more as a result.

SHAPING RELATIONSHIPS AND DECISIONS

Strategic conversations don't just solve immediate problems; they shape the trajectory of relationships. Every word, every pause, every acknowledgment contributes to a narrative. In a professional setting, this means fostering partnerships that grow over time rather than fizzling after a single transaction. In personal life it means building relationships where understanding deepens rather than erodes.

Take, for instance, a mentor-mentee relationship. A mentor who lectures without listening risks alienating the mentee. But one who asks thoughtful questions—such as "How do you see your future?" or "What do you think is holding you back?"—creates space for trust and mutual respect. The mentee feels valued, and the mentor gains insight into how they can provide meaningful guidance.

Strategic conversations are not just about what you say but how you position yourself as a partner in problem-solving, whether in personal or professional contexts.

OVERCOMING CHALLENGES THROUGH COMMUNICATION

When challenges arise, empathic communication becomes the difference between escalation and resolution. Imagine leading a team facing a project delay that could jeopardize client trust. Transparency combined with strategic framing is critical.

Begin with acknowledgment: "We're behind schedule. I know this is frustrating, and you probably blame me."

Then, pivot to reassurance and collaboration: "Here's how we're addressing it. I'd love your input on how we can accelerate progress. What stands in our way?"

This approach acknowledges the problem, shows accountability, and invites the other party into the solution while simultaneously focusing their thinking.

Imagine facing the dissatisfied client threatening to terminate

a major account because of delay. Instead of defending your position, use Tactical Empathy.

"It's clear you're angry because our timeline fell short of what we promised. You are probably thinking you should terminate the contract. You're probably asking yourself why you gave it to us in the first place."

Labeling the negative emotions and obvious thoughts diffuses anger. You don't get rid of the elephant in the room by denying it, ignoring it, or offering excuses as to why it's there. You appear to be fearless and accountable when you address the negative head-on by simple acknowledgment without excuses. You become a straight shooter and begin to rebuild trust.

This opens the door for a productive conversation about solutions. This is your best chance of success at salvaging the relationship and the future business.

DEFUSING TENSION AND CREATING CLARITY

Another key Black Swan skill is *labeling*. This is the act of identifying and calling out emotions or concerns, even when they remain unspoken. *Especially* if they remain unspoken.

Labeling is a critical tool in strategic conversations because it helps defuse tension, clarify misunderstandings, and establish a deeper level of trust.

Labeling comes in three basic forms:

First Level: More tentative/exploring. "It seems...It sounds...It looks...It feels like you are (label the dynamic, emotion, or affect change).

Ex: "It seems like you like stability." "It seems like you have a reason for saying that."

Second Level: More probable—insight you should have based on the circumstances. "You're probably angry." "You're probably wondering."

Third Level: When what they are saying is crystal clear. "It's clear you're angry." "It's clear you blame us and are holding me accountable."

This is very much like the continuum used in law enforcement: reasonable suspicion (reason to investigate based on observation, yet uncertainty as to the cause), probable cause (enough reason to make an arrest and take the issue to a trial), guilt beyond a reasonable doubt (the results of the trial).

GUIDING THE CONVERSATION

Calibrated questions are one of the most powerful tools in the Black Swan arsenal, and they're indispensable in strategic conversations. These open-ended, non-accusatory questions are designed to guide the conversation while giving the other party the illusion of control.

These questions are almost exclusively limited to "What?" and "How?"

Strategic conversations often require steering discussions without overtly imposing your agenda. For example, in a leadership meeting where there's resistance to a new initiative, a calibrated question like, "How do you see this change impacting our goals?"

This invites participation and shifts the focus to collaborative problem-solving that is framed on an objective. These questions disarm defensiveness and elicit valuable insights that might otherwise remain hidden.

In the context of uncovering Black Swans, calibrated questions are particularly effective. Questions like, "What's holding you back from moving forward?" or "What's the biggest challenge you're facing in this situation?" can reveal the hidden barriers or motivations that shape the other party's behavior.

You may have noticed that the "What?" question is principally designed to uncover obstacles, and the "How?" question is principally designed to create implementation. Please look again at them to see the difference and experience the impact on thinking.

THE ROLE OF EMOTIONAL INTELLIGENCE IN STRATEGIC CONVERSATIONS

The Black Swan Skills emphasize the importance of emotional intelligence (EQ)—the ability to recognize, understand, and manage your emotions and those of others. Strategic conversations are rarely purely logical; they're deeply influenced by emotions, perceptions, and interpersonal dynamics.

The uncomfortable reality is that "logic" is like beauty—it's in the eye of the beholder. You make decisions based on what you care about, what you value. That makes decision-making, by definition, an emotional process.

There have been a few books that have explored this idea, *Descartes' Error*[1] being the one where I first saw this explained. Without the use of emotion, you can follow directions, but to make a decision is an evaluation. You evaluate based on what's important to you, what you care about, what your values are.

Using Tactical Empathy, labeling, and dynamic silence are all ways to leverage EQ. For instance, recognizing when someone's tone shifts or when their body language changes can alert you to underlying emotions that might not align with their words. Addressing these subtle cues, perhaps by saying, "It seems like there's something else on your mind," can lead to a breakthrough.

In high-stakes scenarios, maintaining emotional control—especially when faced with resistance or hostility—is critical. The ability to stay calm, composed, and focused on your objectives ensures that you can navigate even the most challenging conversations with confidence.

The best strategy to prepare to remain calm? The simple mental rehearsal of imagining yourself remaining calm. The brain science these days illustrates what the top professional athletes have demonstrated from the beginning of sport: The part of your brain that imagines doing something is the same part of your brain that engages when you actually do it.

Mental rehearsal gives you the competitive edge.

THE TRAITS OF EFFECTIVE COMMUNICATORS

What separates effective communicators from the rest is not just the words they use but their ability to adapt, listen, and connect on a human level. Effective communicators:

1. Proactively listen: They focus not just on words but on tone, body language, and subtext. Proactively listening allows them to prepare for and anticipate the unspoken, yet predictable, concerns and address them.

2. Stay calm under pressure: High-stakes situations can trigger defensiveness or aggression. Effective communicators learn to remain composed, using measured responses to help maintain self-control.

3. Ask calibrated questions: Instead of making demands or assumptions, they use calibrated questions to guide conversations and uncover the black swans (hidden information) in the conversation.

THE IMPORTANCE OF DYNAMIC SILENCE IN STRATEGIC CONVERSATIONS

Silence is one of the most underutilized tools in communication. The Black Swan method emphasizes the power of *dynamic silence*—purposeful pauses that create space for reflection and invite the other party to fill the void with critical information.

In strategic conversations, silence can feel uncomfortable, but it's often where breakthroughs happen. Imagine you've just posed a calibrated question to a hesitant client: "What would need to happen for this solution to work for you?"

Instead of rushing to fill the silence, you wait. The pause allows them to think deeply about their response, often revealing insights or concerns they wouldn't have shared otherwise. Dynamic silence turns moments of discomfort into opportunities for discovery.

CONCLUSION: MASTERING STRATEGIC CONVERSATIONS

Strategic conversations are not a means to an end—they are the threads that weave the fabric of relationships to outcomes. By mastering trust-based influence through Tactical Empathy, you create spaces where collaboration thrives and challenges are overcome.

The art of strategic communication demands humility (getting out of your own way), practice, and a willingness to learn. Whether negotiating a deal, resolving conflict, or deepening a relationship, the principles of tactical empathy, labeling, calibrated questioning, and adaptability can transform the way you connect with others. In the end the most impactful conversations leave both parties feeling valued, understood, and ready to move forward together.

ENDNOTE

1.   Antonio Damasio, *Descartes' Error: Emotion, Reason, and the Human Brain* (Penguin Books, 2005).

About Chris

Chris Voss is the best-selling author of *Never Split the Difference*, a former lead international FBI kidnapping negotiator, and the CEO and founder of The Black Swan Group.

During his twenty-four-year career with the FBI, Chris served as the FBI's hostage negotiation representative for the National Security Council's Hostage Working Group and has represented the US at two international conferences. He's been recognized for a number of awards, including the Attorney General's Award, and the FBI Agents Association Award for Distinguished and Exemplary Service. He has received negotiation training from the FBI, Scotland Yard, and Harvard Law School.

Since retiring from the FBI, Chris has earned his master's in public administration from Harvard University and taught at a number of esteemed institutions, including the University of Southern California Marshall School of Business, Georgetown University, Harvard University, Northwestern University, the IMD Business School in Lausanne, Switzerland, and the Goethe Business School in Frankfurt, Germany.

Following the success of his book *Never Split the Difference*, Chris coauthored a book with real estate guru Steve Shull, *The Full Fee Agent*, which provides practical and skillful negotiation techniques for real estate agents—both experienced and expert. Chris has been featured on podcasts and media outlets such as *Time* magazine, CNN, CNBC, the Lex Fridman podcast Inc., and others.

His company, The Black Swan Group, established in 2008, aims at providing negotiation coaching for professionals all over the world through corporate and individual coaching, as well as live events.

When he isn't coaching or giving keynote speeches, Chris is passionate about learning, working out, reading, and spending time with his family. He currently lives in Las Vegas.

To connect with Chris and his company, you can go to blackswanltd.com. You can also follow him on LinkedIn and Instagram.

CHAPTER 2

FIRST PRINCIPLES: START WITH "WHY?"

By Burgundy Morgan

I was thirteen years old the day I ran away.

My childhood had been a cautionary tale that taught me exactly how I didn't want to live. My mother did her best with the limited opportunities available to her, but home life was chaotic, unstable, and rife with poor adult functioning. I wanted out.

Not surprisingly, I discovered that life as a runaway only traded one bad situation for another. I returned home, more determined than ever to find a better way.

By fourteen, I was earning my own money. At fifteen, a foreign student exchange program offered me my first experience in turning adversity into opportunity—what I call "Turning the Terrible into the Terrific," and from sixteen to nineteen, I lived abroad in Ecuador, Peru, and France. I set high goals for myself, but at nineteen, I became pregnant and unhoused, despite my vow to break the generational pattern my mother experienced.

Desperation can be a powerful catalyst. It made me even more resourceful and determined. I relied on my community college's gym for showers, slept in my car in a campus parking lot, stayed with friends when I could, and navigated the dangerous world of emergency shelters.

Overachievement was my way out.

My first mentor, Jenny Peters, founder of Mo' Better Music, believed in me. She encouraged my determination and resourcefulness. Her wise advice launched my early career as a record promoter. At Mo' Better Music we charted hit records and achieved accolades, including a Billboard Music Award for number one chart share. Jenny also supported my decision to expand my skillset and move my base from New York City to Los Angeles to become an intellectual property attorney focusing on music, film, television, and new media. It was an exciting time! I was achieving every goal I'd set. In February 2003 I opened my own law firm in Beverly Hills.

One month later I came an inch away from death.

The Hit I Never Saw Coming

It's a sound I'll never forget—metal shrieking against metal, glass exploding, and the violent impact. It was a multicar pileup. In an instant my entire life changed.

I was grateful to be alive, but it would be a year and a half before I could walk properly again. Before the accident, I worked with some of the biggest names in the entertainment industry. After the accident, I couldn't even dial the phone. Among my other injuries, I sustained a brain injury with symptoms similar to a stroke that affected my motor function. The left side of my body, my coordination, and my gait were impaired. More than one doctor suggested I find a less rigorous career or go on permanent disability. To prepare me for long rehabilitation with uncertain outcomes, the doctors had essentially given me a pass on life: I could quit everything, and no one would think less of me for it. The easy path was clear, but the greatest growth comes from the hardest climb, even when each small step feels like a mile—and there my healing journey began.

Wayne Dyer said, "Don't die with your music still in you." I was still alive. I had to pivot and adapt to my new circumstances. I decided to learn everything I could about neuroplasticity and cognitive rehabilitation. I learned to retrain my brain by forming new neural pathways to compensate for damaged areas, kind of like traffic being re-routed after an accident.

I also dove into the wisdom movement. I learned from thinkers such as Tony Robbins, Peter Diamandis, and Dr. Don Beck. I was inspired by organizations such as X-PRIZE and the Genius Network community. The result was a new version of me that still had drive but prioritized new ways of thinking, embracing empathy, connection, meaningful contribution, and wisdom.

What do wisdom, empathy, and connection have to do with being a lawyer?

Everything.

THE GIFT, AND CURSE, OF TIME

My brush with death left me with a profound appreciation for time. Time is a finite, precious resource. Now, I'm highly selective with projects because one day I'll die, but I don't know when.

It might sound bleak, but it's not. To me, inevitable death is a wise and kind reminder to be grateful for every experience—even *really* challenging ones. Time and death are catalysts for clarity. They enable me to examine my motivations with courageous honesty: What do I *really* want? *Why* do I want it? What's *important*?

This awareness helped me be a strong advocate for my clients too, especially when a deal initially seems too good to pass up.

Over the course of my career, I have contributed my music expertise to major recording artists, projects with Disney, Netflix, Prime, HBO, and for feature films including the Spiderman franchise, Dune, The Greatest Showman and its Grammy winning soundtrack album, alongside ethical caring attorneys like Bill Skrzyniarz and Tanya Mallean.

Entertainment and media contracts are generally *not* short-term transactions. For example, a major record label recording agreement could last a decade or longer. Songwriter publishing deals are often for the life of the *copyright*, which is longer than the life of the *songwriter*.

As such, many entertainment contracts are like a marriage. And like some marriages, some deals should never happen! In any strategic negotiation, analysis is crucial, and I created a helpful toolkit for decision-making to ensure the project is values aligned and the people are a good team fit.

I'll share my Yes Test Toolkit for decision-making, but first, let's begin with a case study that demonstrates its value.

MAKE THE RIGHT DEAL FOR THE RIGHT REASONS

I was leading a high-stakes negotiation on behalf of a young rising-star client. This client had growing success in film and TV and began releasing music on social media for fun.

A renowned record company noticed the social media buzz and offered a five-album deal. Initially, my client was flattered and delighted by the offer. Yet after applying the Yes Test Toolkit, ultimately, the "juice wasn't worth the squeeze." A five-album deal could last more than a decade, and recording obligations could interfere with their ability to readily accept subsequent opportunities. Income generated by film and television was already much higher than the income anticipated from the record deal. Although the offer was enticing, decision tools revealed that implementation would be problematic. My client politely declined the offer, electing to continue to write songs for fun and release music independently, preserving both time-freedom and flexibility.

Shortly after my client declined the record deal, they landed a leading role in a multi-year feature film franchise. Although tempted by the allure of music stardom, decision tools provided clarity, saved them from an overpacked schedule, exhaustion, and burnout. Importantly, saying no gave room to say yes to a more lucrative opportunity.

Sometimes it's tough to walk away from a tantalizing offer, but decision tools, like those in my Yes Test Toolkit, cut through the allure to reveal deeper truths. And that's exactly why we need it.

If one has clarity on *what* they want and *why* they want it, gracefully declining an opportunity for the right reasons opens the door to more aligned projects later.

Remember, we're not always going to get it right. When I think about navigating life's most important interactions, I think of Maya Angelou's quote: "Do the best you can until you know better. Then when you know better, do better."

THE YES TEST TOOLKIT

Two of my most trusted tools in my Yes Test Toolkit come from Joe Polish and Tony Robbins. Both are quick and easy ways to decide if a project is worth your time and commitment.

1. Joe Polish's E.L.F. vs. H.A.L.F. experience: I ask myself, "Is this project Easy, Lucrative, and Fun? Or is it Hard, Annoying, Lame, and Frustrating?"

This tool is simple, easy to remember, and offers instant clarity.

2. Tony Robbins' Level 4 Experience: Does the project satisfy *all* four criteria: Is it good for me? Is it good for others? Does it serve a greater good? And finally, does it feel good?

When a project meets *all* four conditions, it's a resounding yes! If a project is only good for *me* but not for others, and serves no greater good, it's a no! If a project falls short for *me* but serves the greater good, is good for others, and I enjoy the work, but requires extensive, unpaid time (such as nonprofit projects), I will often accept, but with clarity about the trade-offs.

THE GUT CHECK

The Gut Check is another vitally important Yes Test Tool, one that I ignored at my own peril. In fact, I didn't understand the inherent wisdom of gut feelings for *years*.

It was only after I learned that "gut feelings" are associated with the brain's limbic system—which *predates* the brain's language centers—that I realized I'd been ignoring an ancient communication pathway simply because *feelings* didn't seem like an objective basis for decision-making. I still have a strong bias for decision making based on facts and data, but now I listen to my gut, too.

The Gut Check starts with giving yourself the space to *feel* the decision. When you think about moving forward with this project or with a potential business partner, do you feel a sense of ease, excitement, and calm? Or does your body react with tension or dread? Pay attention to any tightness in your chest or knots in your stomach. These signals are your body's way of telling you something isn't right.

After that, mentally walk yourself through the scenario as if you've already decided. Imagine living with the consequences of it—how do you feel a week, a month, or even a year from now? Did the decision bring reassurance or regret? Trusting these imagined responses can be a powerful indicator of which path to choose.

Your gut often knows what's best long before your mind catches up. Listening to it can save you from making choices that look good on paper but will lead you further away from your authentic self.

THE MULTIVERSE METAPHOR

George Bernard Shaw said, "The single biggest problem with communication is the illusion it occurred in the first place."

I have seen business and personal relationships end in disaster due to the *illusion* of agreement. My personal definition of communication is "an exchange of information for *mutual* understanding." Nowadays, I never assume that someone is on the same page. It's crucial to ask questions and remain open and curious for a deeper understanding of another's perspective.

This practice led me to develop a tool I call The Multiverse Metaphor™. The multiverse concept from theoretical physics asks whether different versions of reality exist parallel to our own. To me, it's an apt metaphor for people's vastly different perspectives and opinions. We all process information through our own unique filter of beliefs, cultural conditioning, heuristics, biases, and more. The result? It's as if each of us is experiencing life in our own unique version of reality.

The Multiverse Metaphor™ is a process that prioritizes curiosity over judgment to nurture mutual understanding and empathy. Ask, "What filters, worldviews, and beliefs does the other person have that shape their reality and worldview?" and "What are *mine*?" Assumptions and unspoken expectations damage relationships. Understanding another's worldview leads to better questions, understanding, appreciation, and respect for their unique perspective. By meeting people where they're at, seeing it from their point of view, and walking a mile in their shoes, we approach a mutual understanding. Then, it becomes clear much faster where people are aligned—and where they're not.

The more questions we ask, the more likely we are to make deals that lead to success and avoid those that lead to a courtroom!

THE HUMAN EXPERIENCE: EMBRACING ALL OF IT

Some years after my car accident I met the most amazing human who shaped my life in profound and meaningful ways. Initially, he didn't strike me as my "type" for a romantic partner. (I'm usually attracted to the smartest person in the room, which unfortunately sometimes comes with a side of arrogance.) But this person was my favorite flavor of smart: He was *wise*, lighthearted, patient, and above all, kind. It was very clear early on that I had met the love of my life. We married, full of hope for a long, joyful future together. But the future we looked forward to would never be.

My beloved was diagnosed with terminal brain cancer.

He was diagnosed with Glioblastoma (grade IV). A six-centimeter brain tumor caused seizures, impaired vision, and impaired motor skills. His bright future as a firefighter and paramedic was never going to happen. Yet he never lost his ability to create empowering meaning even during the toughest life challenges, at one point saying, "Look at the bright side. Who knew I'd retire this *young*!"

As we navigated the reality of our new circumstances during this extremely difficult time, we committed to 'Turning the Terrible into the Terrific.' We talked *a lot* about lessons learned from my car accident, poor prognosis, and an uncertain future. The parallels were not lost on us. I had been through this before.

Because I had not given up after my car accident, I had gained the knowledge, skill, and experience to help the person I loved most find a new path forward with grace. We both had a profound realization that hardships are Teachable Moments that can bring unexpected gifts and that life's greatest challenges are opportunities to become *more*. It was an epiphany—the kind of clarity that stays with me to this day, profound and deeply transformative.

There are no words to describe the raw pain of grief I experienced following my beloved's eventual death. But before he died, we promised to *never* give up on what's important, to keep loving, learning, laughing, and knowing that life is about getting it right—and getting it terribly wrong. It's about success and failure, joy and despair, wins and losses, and *everything* in between. The human experience is about embracing *all* of it.

And as spiritual leader Ram Dass so eloquently said, "We're all just walking each other home."

TIME TO CHOOSE WISELY

It might seem uncommon that a "lawyer" prioritizes empathy and connection, but I don't work with cases, I work with *humans*. We are all navigating life the best we can in the time we have. We can all be gentle mirrors for each other, as teachers and students both.

We all have a soul-deep desire for meaning, purpose, and joy. Will we spend our hours on the trivial and meaningless, or on things that spark resonance within our soul? Will we spend our time in conversations that foster connection or sow discord? Yes, this requires reflection and work. I promise it's worth it. How we spend our time is like spending a coin from a limited purse. Let's choose wisely.

About Burgundy

Burgundy Morgan, Esq.
Attorney, Educator, Author, Musician
www.burgundymorgan.com

*"Empowering doers and dreamers who want
to change the world for the better."*

Burgundy's mission is to empower those who not only seek success but who strive to leave a legacy that uplifts humanity.

A polymath and techno-optimist with decades of experience in intellectual property, Burgundy helps visionaries and do-gooders navigate the ever-evolving intersection of technology, creativity, and law while staying grounded in ethical principles. Burgundy provides a unique blend of legal and business acumen with heartfelt support and guidance for clients, fostering lasting relationships built on connection and trust.

Intellectual Property, Innovation, and Entertainment

Burgundy understands the unique challenges individuals, businesses, and creative professionals face when navigating a complex legal landscape and fosters a collaborative environment where clients can discuss their concerns openly. Tailored solutions minimize risks and maximize potential to transform uncertainty into clarity. With straightforward, practical legal solutions, Burgundy provides peace of mind—serving as a trusted adviser for those who dare to dream big.

Burgundy's extensive legal experience covers all facets of the entertainment and education industry, including new media and technology applications. With a track record that includes notable film, television, music, and live events, Burgundy serves as a resourceful attorney for copyright and trademark law matters, licensing agreements, distribution agreements, and rights and clearances, among other key contributions.

Burgundy is a respected adviser to artists, musicians, music producers, filmmakers, composers, production companies, publishers, record labels, live event and festival producers, podcasters, authors, speakers, educators, thought leaders, entrepreneurs, new media innovators, life and business coaches, social media influencers, and inspirational content creators.

A futurist, Burgundy works with forward-thinking innovators to ethically integrate new technologies so humanity can embrace these advancements with enthusiasm. The through-line is that Burgundy passionately supports those who are innovative and heart-driven, helping bright minds with big hearts bring their most impactful ideas to life. Burgundy *helps helpers* who are doing work that *matters*.

Harmony in Law and Life

Burgundy Morgan is a graduate of Pepperdine University School of Law. A former professional musician with two undergraduate degrees in music, Burgundy plays guitar, bass guitar, and piano. Music remains a core passion.

Beyond professional achievements, Burgundy finds joy in nature, music, transformational festival culture, and exploring the intersection of spirituality and science. Burgundy is a "lifelong learner" dedicated to personal growth and inclusive systems-level thinking—leveraging technology to deepen human wisdom and understanding.

CHAPTER 3

NAVIGATING THREATS IN NEGOTIATIONS

The Blueprint for Taking Back Control

By Thorsten Hofmann

"I f you don't do what I say right away, she won't survive! I swear it!"

The anger in his voice was unmistakable, but I could also hear the hint of uncertainty. He pressed the knife firmly to the neck of the young woman, who knelt in front of him with wide-open eyes. She was his neighbor, a young woman he had apparently known for a long time. Her blond hair fell untidily over her shoulders, and she trembled with fear.

He took a step back, the knife still in his hand. "I have nothing left to lose," he murmured as he looked nervously over his shoulder. The hostage, his neighbor, had her eyes tightly closed, as if she wanted to block out reality. I knew that she knew him from many chance encounters in the stairwell or on the street—a fleeting greeting, a few words about the weather, perhaps. Now her life hung by a thread.

"I understand you're desperate," I continued. "But she's not your enemy. She is someone you know, who trusts you." I labeled his emotions to establish a relationship with him. It was clear that he was emotionally unstable, and I had to calm him down in some way.

"I just want to get out of here," he finally said, his voice now quieter. "But no one helps me."

"I'm here to help you," I answered. "I understand that you want to talk about a solution to the current situation." I reduced the threat and went back to the topic of the negotiation. I spoke calmly, trying to give him a sense of control, while at the same time steering him towards the first step of a peaceful solution.

And I am working to save her life.

THREATS ARE OMNIPRESENT

Negotiation can save lives, resolve conflict situations, turn conflicting interests into solutions, turn opponents into partners, and make everyone's life more successful. Life *is* negotiation.

I never expected to be in that kind of high stakes, life or death situation.

I have been working in operational crisis management, as a crisis negotiator and in crisis communication for over thirty years—initially at the Federal Criminal Police Office (BKA) and the Interpol National Central Bureau (NCB) in Germany, and later as managing director of my company, which specializes in strategic crisis communication and negotiation. I have experienced and managed a wide variety of cases in a wide range of sectors at first hand. The spectrum ranges from kidnappings (tourists, managers, ship crews or employees of aid organizations abroad) and extortion, including with contaminated food, to interrogations of serious criminals in organized crime, conflicts between companies and citizens' initiatives, trade union negotiations and many negotiations in politics, through to online extortion with stolen or falsified data. I have repeatedly tested the effectiveness of a wide variety of negotiation techniques and tactics and have never stopped developing myself. The more I got involved in this field, the more it fascinated me. Negotiation is also my life. Strategic conversations are the cornerstone of my entire career.

Over the past three decades through my training and extensive field experience, I've learned that in most tense conversations, there is almost always a moment in which a threat is delivered.

In international politics the EU threatens China with higher taxes if subsidies are not reduced. In the business world, a company threatens to end its business relationship with a supplier or service provider if conditions are not improved or certain requirements are not met. In a relationship, one partner threatens to end the relationship or leave the apartment if the other does not change certain behaviors or make concessions.

Threats can show up anywhere at any time.

Even "reasonable" people can become opponents in negotiations: a teenage daughter can be charming one moment and insulting you the next. Your boss can be cooperative most of the time, but suddenly make an "irrational" demand on a Friday afternoon and garnish it with a threat. A long-standing customer could suddenly threaten to take their business elsewhere if you refuse to give them a discount.

Your ability to navigate a conversation that turns threatening might not always spell the difference between life and death, but it can help you to diffuse tension, restore balance and ultimately, get what you want from the exchange.

So, how do you deal with it? How do you respond if someone is threatening to walk away, file a lawsuit, or damage your reputation?

You follow these steps.

DON'T LET THEM HIJACK YOUR AMYGDALA

When faced with an irrational negotiator the key is to act deliberately, not just *react*. The second you allow yourself to be triggered, you lose the upper hand. It's vital that you take control of your emotions and breathing is a powerful tool for managing impulse control.

The Navy SEALs call this technique "arousal control." It's not what you might think—it's about using breathing to regulate the body's physiological arousal, specifically the fight, flight, or freeze response. Breathing connects the sympathetic nervous system, which triggers our stress response, and the parasympathetic nervous system, which calms us down afterward.

When the sympathetic nervous system is activated, hormones like cortisol, adrenaline, and norepinephrine flood the body, preparing it for a strong reaction to danger. But in today's world, where we aren't being chased by saber tooth tigers and threats are often intangible, this response can be counterproductive. Without the ability to regulate these systems, we may act impulsively in situations where clear thinking is essential.

By mastering your breath, you regain control of your physiological response, allowing you to approach even the most intense negotiations with clarity and composure.

REDUCE THE THREAT

A threat always has something behind it, and it's your job as the negotiator to uncover what that is. However, under no circumstances should a threat be ignored or repeated. Repeating it only solidifies the threat at the negotiating table, while ignoring it makes the other party feel dismissed, which can lead to even greater aggression.

Even worse than ignoring a threat is responding with a counterthreat. This shifts the negotiation from the issues to the relationship, edging both parties toward a destructive endgame.

So how do you respond when someone says, "If I don't get a 10 percent discount immediately, I'll de-list your company"? You might say, "If I understand you correctly, you're considering various alternatives based on new conditions. Let's focus on finding a solution that benefits us both."

This allows you to think before reacting and to replace ultimatums with alternatives.

DIAGNOSE THE THREAT

Sometimes threats are direct, but other times, they are more subtle. Someone might say, "You know, I'd be very sorry if this hurts your reputation." Regardless, it is important that you understand what triggered the threat. The first step to effective threat diagnosis is to physically and/or psychologically remove yourself from the situation.

You could suggest to your counterpart that it's time for a break to take the "steam" out of the situation.

You can imagine that you are an external observer trying to assess the threat more objectively. This so-called dissociated behavior causes you to detach yourself from the situation. In doing so, you reduce your emotions (which keeps your amygdala from being hijacked) and you can really hear what the other side is saying. Next, consider the motivation behind the threat, which can identify the threatener as one of these types:

The victim: If your counterpart felt frustrated or offended, the threat may have arisen from a basic psychological need to be heard and acknowledged.

The insecure: The insecure person simply doesn't know how to negotiate with you or hasn't learned the skills to do so. The only thing he can do is threaten. Help him negotiate.

The direct one: This person informs you directly of the actual constraints they face or the strong external alternatives they have. He brings this to the table aggressively linguistically but will also be solution-oriented in the search for options.

The bluffer: He tries to test your dependence on the business/topic. If this is the case, then the threat is more tactical than realistic. If you react too quickly by giving in, he'll assume he's "won" control.

If you can assess the root of the threat, you are in a much better position to respond to it.

STEER THE NEGOTIATION TO SAFE GROUND

The Spanish writer José Bergamin once said, "Advice always contains an implicit threat, just as a threat always contains implicit advice." Your job as a negotiator is to discover the implicit advice within a "threat."

Imagine a contractor threatens to sue you as a supplier over a proposed change in the delivery date for raw materials. You can try to find out the motivation for the threat by asking, for example, "Why might a lawsuit be a better option for you than continuing our conversations?" "What could be the disadvantages of a lawsuit compared with continuing our talks?"

If your negotiator reveals that he expects the courts to rule in his favor, his threat is based on his sense of subjectively perceived power. Finally, if you inquire about the exact type of lawsuit he wants to file, you will be able to determine if the threat could cause you real harm, if it is already thought out, or if it is more of a bluff. If, on the other hand, your counterpart says that your delays could bankrupt their company, you can negotiate a realistic restriction.

Using different question tactics such as circular questions, alternative questions, or vision questions are a powerful way to bring hidden information to the surface.

The goal here is always to determine the subjective power or actual limitations that are behind the threat. Once you have asked enough questions to understand their motivation you can present an alternative that speaks directly to it.

LABEL THE NEGOTIATION A THREAT

If a threat is simply a tactic to intimidate you, your response should be firm. If, after analyzing the situation, you realize the other party is bluffing, let them know that you're not interested in negotiating this way. You could say, "I take this as a threat, and I don't find threats productive. Let's work together to find a solution."

This is called labeling a threat, and it helps neutralize negative intentions while giving you more control. Research by Anne L. Lytle, Jeanne M. Brett, and Debra L. Shapiro shows that labeling the situation—pointing out what's happening—can effectively get a negotiation back on track when threats are involved. By doing this, you create the same emotional distance for your counterpart that you've gained by diagnosing the threat.

You also create accountability. You're on to them, you're not afraid, and now they know it!

BE READY TO WALK AWAY

Sometimes, despite your best efforts, your counterpart will only respond to a firm boundary. In such cases, issuing a "walk-away" can enhance your credibility and help refocus the discussion on shared interests to avoid deadlock. Research by Lytle, Brett, and Shapiro shows that combining assertiveness with cooperation is highly effective in negotiations. From my experience in crisis negotiations at the Federal Criminal Police Office and Interpol, I can confirm this in practice.

If the other party continues to use threats, you should give a clear warning that there is a limit. You might be wondering: isn't a warning just another threat? The difference lies in the wording and tone. The same statement can have completely different effects depending on how it's communicated. A threat assigns blame, which destroys the relationship and leads to a spiral of accusations. A warning, however, maintains empathy and sets boundaries without attacking the other party.

Furthermore, a threat targets a person directly. For example, saying, "If you don't stop threatening, this negotiation will fail" places the blame for failure squarely on the other party. The natural response is to reject that blame, leading to a back-and-forth exchange of accusations, which derails the conversation.

A warning, on the other hand, looks ahead to a potential breakdown in negotiations, but without assigning blame. It offers the other party a sense of control. For example, in a conversation with a client, you might say, "We've made a lot of progress, but I'm concerned about whether we'll be able to continue this discussion."

Then, deliver the crucial line—clearly and calmly: "Have you given up on this negotiation?" Avoid overexplaining, and let the sentence stand on its own. Now they know that you are prepared to walk away, and the question forces them to justify their actions without feeling attacked. After all, who wants to admit they're giving up?

By framing it this way, you avoid blame and leave the door open for them to re-engage in the negotiation. You position yourself as their ally, not their adversary. Whether you are negotiating with a hostage taker or a toddler, threats create resistance and turn negotiations into battles. Warnings, on the other hand, create opportunities to work toward a shared goal.

WE'RE ALL HUMAN

After working for years with the Federal Criminal Police in Germany, I started my own company, which I sold in 2022. Though I am financially independent now, I act as managing director of a scientific Institute for Negotiation at the Quadriga University of Applied Sciences in Berlin, continuing to research what drives a strategic conversation. My passion for this work is as strong as ever because I feel that everyone can benefit from mastering the art of negotiation.

What we must remember is that everyone involved in a negotiation is a human being, and human behavior is often predictable. In every negotiation, both parties have a goal and behind that goal is a specific motivation.

Threats are defaulted to when someone lacks the ability to communicate their desires. It's a cry to be understood. Demands are just the words that stand in front of the true need. If we can retain control of our emotions and respond from the field of our intellect, we can ask the questions that lead to the answers we're looking for.

As I look back on the many negotiations I've faced—whether in life-or-death situations or with a customer-service agent—the lessons remain the same. Behind every threat is a human being grappling with their own fears. What they need is not dominance but understanding, not power but partnership.

In the heat of a negotiation, it's easy to get caught in the firestorm of words and emotions, but our greatest power lies in staying calm, asking questions, and uncovering what's truly driving the other person's behavior.

At the end of the day, it isn't about who wins or loses. It's about how we navigate our differences to find a solution that works for both sides and to build bridges, not walls.

That, more than anything, is the true power of negotiation.

About Thorsten

Thorsten Hofmann leads the scientific institute C4 Center for Negotiation at the Quadriga University, Berlin. He is an internationally certified Negotiation Trainer and advises corporations and organizations in complex negotiation processes. As a former investigator to the German Federal Criminal Police Office (Bundeskriminalamt, BKA) and Interpol he operated in the field of organized crime and worked on some of the most spectacular cases of extortions and kidnappings. Thorsten Hofmann looks back on more than thirty years of negotiation experience in different areas and branches. He studied economics, psychology, and behavior analysis. Furthermore, he is a graduate of the Federal Academy for Security Policy (Bundesakademie für Sicherheitspolitik, BAKS), the highest-ranking interagency advanced-education facility on the federal public level.

Thorsten Hofmann advises, among others, corporations, organizations, and executive managers in the field of negotiations and writes commentaries on current negotiation processes for relevant branches and mass media outlets from a scientific perspective. As an internationally demanded speaker, he teaches negotiation techniques, as well as crisis, risk and conflict communication skills.

The C4 Center for Negotiation offers extensive seminars and certification programs in the field of negotiations and negotiation management with the goal to provide a contribution to the optimization of negotiation outcomes for individuals, teams, corporations, and political organizations.

Learn more:

www.c4-quadriga.eu/en

www.negotiation-blog.eu

CHAPTER 4

THE PARIENTE PRINCIPLES

How to Win Any Argument with Strategic Empathy

By Michael Pariente

"They're going to kill me."

I had almost ignored the ringing of the phone but decided at the last minute to answer when I saw that it was a client calling.

"The police are here, and they're going to shoot."

Sweat trickled down my face as I raced through the Las Vegas heat to my client's house.

Twenty police cars surrounded the property, lights flashing as officers made their way through the front door, guns drawn and ready for whatever might await them inside. I talked my way through and climbed the stairs to the master bedroom, where my client was barricaded inside.

The tension was thick, and I found myself in the eye of the storm, standing between my client and the police. He was behind me, gun in hand, close enough that I could feel his breath on my back. The gun wasn't pointed at me, but the threat was real, and so was my responsibility. I was here to represent him, to diffuse this standoff, and to ensure that no one left the scene in a body bag. I had to negotiate my way through this delicate balance, keeping the police at bay while convincing my client to lower the gun and trust me to guide him through this dark moment.

It had started as a domestic dispute between my client and his mother. I was used to tension as a criminal defense attorney, but usually I was negotiating inside the safety of a courtroom and not with multiple guns pointed in my direction.

This was a landmark case that had made it all the way to the Supreme Court of Nevada. I had argued that a defendant charged with domestic battery had a right to a jury trial because they would lose their Second Amendment rights if found guilty by a judge alone.

This was vitally important legislation for reasons too deep to fit into this chapter, but I remember thinking that if I died that day but had changed the law, I was ok with it. I spoke to my client very calmly in my best FM radio DJ voice and reassured him that no one was going to shoot him. I explained his fear to the police and explained the police's point of view to my client. I presented an alternative and we agreed on a summons to appear in court rather than an arrest.

Eventually, the situation diffused, the cops left, and the case resulted in what has been called "the most significant Nevada Supreme Court Case of the 21st Century!" That case put me on the map and my ability to change the law and to negotiate what could have been a disastrous situation resulted in my becoming one of the most sought-after attorneys in Nevada.

What strikes me as funny now, is that I wasn't even trying to do anything spectacular. I just wanted to protect my client.

Now I realize that the strategies I was deploying are components of Chris Voss' principle of tactical empathy, but I didn't call it that back then.

I was just trying to win cases and on the morning of that police standoff, I was just trying to get out of there alive.

I realize now that my success over the years had little to do with what I learned in law school and everything to do with what I learned at home.

EMPATHY IN ACTION

A couple of years ago I got a call from my father. He had received an email from an executive producer of the hit show *This Is Us*. The email had come from a yahoo account, and considering that no one I knew still used yahoo, I told him to disregard it as spam.

A few weeks later that same producer tracked me down. It turns out they were shooting scenes set in 2020 and their characters were going to be using Zoom. They got curious about who invented facetime technology and discovered my father's Wikipedia page. Back in the 1970s my dad invented the algorithm that Zoom and other facetime platforms use today. Unfortunately, he never patented it, so when Covid hit and the world began to run on facetime, he never saw a dime.

We set up a meeting and the producers liked my parents so much they ended up featuring their story on episode 8 of season 5. That night, my father was trending on Twitter! A few weeks ago, I traveled to Stanford University to accept an award on his behalf from the founder of Zoom. I'm sure the audience, all tech executives, wanted to hear the story about how this life-changing algorithm was invented, but the truth was I have no idea. I knew my dad was a genius, but what I was interested in sharing with them is how his intellect paled in comparison to his empathy.

As a minority in a small town in Kansas, my family and I experienced our share of racism. I was bullied, prank called and harassed even in elementary school. I vividly remember flipping through a toy catalog and spotting a bright red fire truck. My birthday was coming up, so I took the catalog to my dad, he flipped through it and handed it back to me.

"We won't be buying anything from this catalog," he said gently. "There isn't a single child in these pictures of an ethnic minority."

At first, I didn't care. I wanted that firetruck! What I came to understand however, was that underrepresentation is what, in part, leads to racism and bullying. People fear what they aren't familiar with.

His explanation, which I'll never forget, taught me that my empathy must be deep rooted and nondiscriminatory. My empathy must extend to people who were different from me, even those who bullied me, for they were acting out of fear and misinformation and needed my guidance, not my wrath.

I believe this deep-rooted empathy is what led me to pursuing a career as a criminal defense attorney, a job that requires me to defend people others find abhorrent.

In fact, I've lost count of how many times people have asked me how I sleep at night knowing I'm defending the guilty. One time, I visited a school to speak at Career Day and one of the other speakers was a firefighter. He asked me how I defend someone I know is guilty.

"What if you know someone is guilty of murder?" he asked. "How do you stand there and defend them?

Everyone judges like that until it's their own kid barricaded in the house and surrounded by police!

I said to him, "You're a fireman. Your job is to save people not to judge them. If a house was burning down with a guy inside, are you going to stop and google him to see what kind of person he is or are you going to charge in and save him? What if you knew the person inside was a child predator? Would you let him burn? No. You'd go get him. Because that's your job."

And this is my job.

Under the label of "criminal" is a label I will always find infinitely more important: *human*. Now of course there are terrible people. There are also good people who become desperate. I would imagine that I am able to defend the guilty for the same reason Chris Voss was able to speak with empathy to a guy holding ten people hostage—because that's the assignment.

And because no one, even a criminal, wants to be judged by the worst mistake they ever made in their most desperate moments.

Does everyone deserve empathy? I have met some horrible people so I can safely say that while not everyone *deserves* empathy, everyone *responds* to it.

I happen to have learned empathy from my parents, but it's a skillset that anyone can practice and learn.

Just like you'd learn to play the guitar, there are a set of steps you can learn to cultivate empathy. The difference is that learning to play "Stairway to Heaven" in A minor probably won't save your life.

Strategic empathy just might.

Here are two of my favorite ways to use it, and to *win*.

THE POWER ALTERNATIVE

One of the most effective and empathetic negotiation strategies I've learned over the years is that of the Power Alternative.

Years ago I represented a client who had an old warrant for a felony drug charge reaching all the way back to the 1970s. To avoid facing the music, he went to a cemetery and found the tombstone of a child and assumed the child's identity. Years later, he ended up working for a Fortune 500 company, and with his fake name was able to get a passport, buy a home and make a lot of money from government contracts. You can imagine that once the government put two and two together, they were livid and determined to see my client serve his jail time.

So, who's right and who's wrong in this case? Hard to say. Yes, my client broke the law and stole someone's identity, but the government totally missed it, which made me wonder what else they might be missing and how vulnerable we really are.

I knew they wanted him to go to jail, so when it was time to negotiate, I went in and stated their wishes before they could.

"It sounds like you already have an idea of how to resolve the case." (This made them feel that they were in the power position.)

At this point I got very curious about their motivation and realized that while they wanted to make my client pay, there was a bigger "why" at play.

The government had screwed up. They had egg on their face and wanted this to go away before it received media coverage and discredited the federal prosecutor and top officials of the governmental agencies involved. I could empathize with that.

I didn't bring up the mistakes they had made as that would have led to them becoming defensive and unwilling to listen.

I proposed that instead of serving jail time, my client pay a fine. There was no negotiating them from five years in jail down to two. I didn't even mention jailtime. I went in with a powerful alternative that I knew met their core desire...making their own mistakes disappear!

A strategic alternative is not a different version of an already proposed solution, but a new solution entirely. Presenting an alternative showed the federal prosecutor that we understood the need for my client to pay in some way. We simply proposed a different form of payment that kept my client out of jail, and appeased the government's need for quiet retribution.

In less than five minutes a case that had dragged on since the 1970s was put to bed.

IT'S NOT YOU; IT'S ME

One thing human beings have in common is that we all have an aversion to being blamed and criticized. No one likes to feel wrong or incompetent. If someone, a co-worker, a boss, or our spouse points out a mistake, the knee-jerk reaction is to feel attacked, get defensive and either argue or shut down.

Once that happens, any chance of productive communication is temporarily shut down and progress is stalled.

That's why one of my favorite negotiation tactics is being the bad guy.

Even if I haven't made a mistake, if I know I have news or information that the other party isn't going to like, I take the hit.

"You're probably going to hate me after this, but..."

"I'm afraid you won't even want to talk to me after this."

"You'll probably think I'm the biggest jerk in the world."

This approach not only humanizes you, but it disarms the other party, triggers empathy and knocks down defenses. Now, you're not the cocky adversary coming in to make them look bad, but a human being concerned about their feelings and the relationship.

I once had a case in which the client I represented was accused of defrauding the DMV.

The DMV is notoriously difficult to work with and they had no interest in speaking with me. They didn't need to. They had all the evidence they needed for a conviction. The good news was that evidence had been grossly mishandled.

I could have called the prosecutor and listed all the mistakes she made in processing. Instead, I said, "You're going to hate me, and I'm terribly sorry, but it turns out that there was a lot of evidence that was improperly submitted and now unusable. It's not your fault. I can't believe the supervisors there don't teach you the right way to do this."

Her guard fell, we worked out a deal and she actually thanked me for saving her from the embarrassment that would have befallen her had she pushed this case further.

This strategy is subtle, but it works. It makes the other party feel like they are in control of what happens next, even if they aren't!

THE MOST PROFITABLE STRATEGY IS FREE!

I watch my competitors throw thousands of dollars away in marketing only to lose the client during intake because they aren't listening. They are rattling on about themselves, the awards they won, and the years they've been in business when the reality is they would close more sales if they shut their mouths!

The client is the main act and the star of the show. The best and most profitable strategies I've ever employed, the ones that have consistently filled my calendar with clients and brought in the most money, don't cost me a dime. It's the power of relationships, authentic connections, and empathetic listening that have proven invaluable—far more than any paid marketing could ever achieve.

As a criminal defense attorney, I've seen firsthand how the

most successful outcomes come not from flashy billboards and dramatic courtroom antics but from truly listening to my clients, understanding their stories, and advocating for them with genuine empathy. This approach has not only been the most profitable strategy for my practice but also the most fulfilling, allowing me to build trust and achieve justice for those who need it most.

I like to think that in my commitment to advocating for truth, leading with empathy and fighting for people who might not "deserve" it, that I am embodying the example my dad set for me. I believe that my success stems from my core beliefs:

That everyone is an imperfect human being entitled to a fair defense...

That I have a job to do and will never let my client's lack of integrity dilute my own...

And that it doesn't matter if you're in a courtroom, a boardroom, or a bedroom—empathy is the secret weapon that strengthens bonds, elevates communication, and ultimately gets you the results you want.

Case closed.

About Michael

Michael Pariente is a dedicated criminal defense attorney and has been passionately defending clients in criminal cases since 1998. His legal career began with roles as a county prosecutor and an assistant federal public defender in El Paso, Texas, before moving to Las Vegas to establish his private practice. Throughout his career, Michael has consistently demonstrated his commitment to protecting the rights of the accused, earning a reputation for his fierce advocacy and legal acumen.

A hallmark of Michael's career is his success in the landmark 2019 case *Andersen v. Eighth Judicial District Court*, which secured the right to jury trials for defendants facing misdemeanor battery domestic violence charges. The *Nevada Independent* hailed the decision as "the most significant Nevada Supreme Court case of the 21st century." Michael's insight on the impact of this decision has also been published in the *Nevada Bar Journal*, further solidifying his status as a thought leader in criminal law.

Michael's roots are as diverse as his career. The son of immigrant parents—his mother from Argentina and his father from India—he grew up appreciating the value of hard work and resilience. His parents met as foreign exchange students at the University of New Mexico, and their story gained a wider audience when they were portrayed by actors on NBC's *This Is Us*, highlighting his father's invention of the algorithm used in video platforms such as Zoom, JPEG, and MPEG.

Michael is driven by a mission to defend against bullies he believes exist within various facets of the justice system, including prosecutors and law enforcement. He sees his role as both a shield and sword for his clients, striving to ensure they are protected and vigorously defended.

While his work is his greatest passion, Michael's dedication extends beyond the courtroom. He attributes much of his professional success to skills he learned from Chris Voss, particularly the use of tactical empathy. Whether negotiating with prosecutors, addressing a jury, or simply listening to a client, Michael ensures that everyone feels heard and understood.

When he's not in the courtroom or the office, Michael pursues his love of drumming, often testing the patience of his wife and neighbors with impromptu sessions at all hours. Though he may struggle to fully discon-nect during vacations, his relentless commitment to his clients and the pursuit of justice is always at the forefront of his life.

CHAPTER 5

ALWAYS FORWARD

"An investment in knowledge pays the best interest."
—Benjamin Franklin

———

By Nico Pesci

P hones fell silent, and across the country seasoned executives sat around polished tables stunned in disbelief, all aware that catastrophe had struck and all wondering how bad it was going to get.

It didn't take long to find out.

Trillions of dollars had evaporated, and the bubble that burst swept the nation, emptying portfolios and destroying legacies. Stone-faced news anchors reported on the gravity of the situation as panic crept into homes across America. 401(k)s...cut in half. Plans for early retirement...wiped out. Decades of working hard to save...wasted.

The fallout was rough, and it left no one untouched. Not even my own parents.

My mother is a highly accomplished author, speaker, and consultant with a PhD from Harvard, and she had dreams of leaving a substantial inheritance to her kids and grandkids. She found what seemed to be a sound investment that would allow her to do so. Unfortunately, in 2008 she realized that it was all fake. She hadn't been investing in anything at all. It was a Ponzi scheme, and the money was gone. The realization that she'd been duped completely altered her identity. It was devastating to watch.

My father, the son of immigrants who came to this country

from Northern Italy in 1921, was the first of his family to attend high school. A highly intelligent man, he was granted a full academic scholarship to both Notre Dame and Marquette where he received a master's degree. For a lot of immigrants, money is an emotional currency. My father was taught to be frugal, and even in his seventies felt that he needed to keep working hard. He was not well-informed about his options and that lack of clarity, coupled with the scarcity mindset that plagued a lot of immigrants, caused him to be afraid to stop working at all.

Seeing my parents navigate this loss and confusion was a gut-wrenching wake-up call. They eventually recovered, but it struck me how tightly our identity is tied to our security. It was clear that for most people, the finish line that once seemed far away was looming closer, and not enough people were ready for it.

So, in 2009, right after the financial crisis, I did something radical and started the one kind of business no one was starting in 2009—a retirement consulting firm.

I had no background in it but had worked in banking and was smart enough to understand how to guide people to a more secure future. I decided then to do whatever I could to make sure no other family had to suffer the same fate my parents had; I would make sure no one else's father had to work on their 80th birthday.

I would help as many senior citizens as I could turn everything they worked for into everything they wanted. In fact, that became the slogan of my new company.

PEOPLE FIRST

My dad grew up in the Bronx in the 1930s. One morning my grandfather woke him up, walked him to Grand Central Station and took him into the men's room. He said, "Son, tell me what you see and hear."

My father looked around, naturally confused. Then my grandfather said, "If anyone ever talks down to you, picture this bathroom. In here, everyone is the same."

Not only did this lesson instill confidence in my father, but it taught him that underneath every title, economic status or degree, we're all human, and I was raised to understand that the janitor deserved the same amount of respect as the CEO.

That sense of empathy is ingrained in me and informs everything I do. Years ago, I was asked to be on a panel at an industry conference in Switzerland. I could have walked on stage and spoken about which funds to invest in, but instead, I focused my talk on trust and empathy. I firmly believe that those two things are the cornerstone of any successful business conversation, particularly in my field. I must be able to help people see what's possible; and I must do it well enough that they trust me to manage their hard-earned money and to craft a plan that gives them the confidence they deserve and the retirement they've earned.

Years ago, the relationship between client and adviser was strictly transactional. The adviser was a tool, a kind of mechanical bridge linking the client to the market. Today, clients are more discerning. Financial markets are more complex. Fear is at an all-time high again and if I can't cultivate trust, my phone will stop ringing.

First, I practice non-judgment. Everyone that comes to me is doing the best they can with what they have and what they know. I meet folks who have just a few thousand dollars to folks with ten million or more, and they get the same respect and attention.

I think of my parents and the fact that every person sitting across from me is someone's mom or dad. I listen to their desires and repeat them back to affirm that I understand their fears and wishes. My goal is not to negotiate with the client, but *for* the client and their dreams.

It's easy in business negotiations to get caught up in our own agenda but that's a mistake. If everyone at the table saw each other not as sets of opposing data but as *people*, success comes much faster.

Too many of the big firms focus on money changing hands and

forget that behind those dollars and account numbers are living, breathing human beings.

How Did We Get Here?

Have you ever gotten in your car, driven to your destination lost in thought and then had no memory of the drive? You might wonder how you even got there.

"How did we get here?" is a question that comes up a lot with clients. Sometimes, it's asked in celebration as clients review their portfolio and are stunned to see so many zeroes. Other times, it's asked in despair as people realize that they'll more than likely outlive their money.

It's this question that prompted me to build a framework around the concept of "retiring forward," which is based on the idea that to build security, continued momentum is key. Most of us have momentum in the working years, tucking away money each paycheck but once we retire, momentum comes to a screeching halt.

That's why it's important to break down a conversation into two parts.

How did you get here? And where would you like to go next?

This is true whether you're discussing retirement, contract negotiation or marriage! It all requires an honest look at what contributes to keeping or losing momentum. If you can get the person on the other side of the table to vulnerably share their story and their goal, you can pinpoint mistakes that were made not for the sake of judgment, but for the sake of being informed and moving in a better direction.

Once I see someone's gaps, I can fill them and prevent them from happening again. I can pull from what they have and determine what they need. Every conversation can benefit from this kind of inventory.

After all, it doesn't matter how badly you want to go somewhere, you aren't getting there without a vehicle and a map.

What Got You Here Won't Get You There

So, now you've got your map, and you're ready to go. The problem is that the map is from 1950. Can you imagine trying to navigate a cross-country trip with a seventy-five-year-old map? Nothing would make sense. New roads that would shorten your route would not be on the map. Cliffs and lakes that have formed over the years would be absent as well, increasing your chances of danger. It may have been the epitome of maps when it was printed in 1950. It may have been given to you by a grandparent and hold sentimental value. Heck, it might be made of gold. But today, as a navigational tool, it's useless to you.

This is what happens when we cling to outdated methods. In my industry, I'm often working to deprogram thirty years of habitual thinking. In some cases, people were so scared of not having enough that they saved aggressively. Now they have more than enough but that scarcity mindset is ingrained, and they're afraid to part with a penny of it. For decades, they received a paycheck every two weeks. They built their whole lives and budgets around two-week periods. Suddenly that two-week routine ends, the paychecks dry up and that change triggers an instinctual feeling of uncertainty. Now, this crippled thinking prevents them from opening their minds to how their investments can create that same steady paycheck.

It's up to me and the team I have built to show them what's possible. Most humans are hardwired to cling to what's familiar. In any strategic conversation, we've got to be able to lead them away from what was and towards what could be.

I often do this by sharing the success stories of others. This kind of social proof and validation works because if we can paint an emotional picture but back it up with logic, we've hit the main points of a solid decision-making framework. Then I invite them into the story.

What might it be like if you got those same results?

Do know what you'd like to do with an extra $100,000, $250,000, or even $500,000?

Painting a vivid picture of what lies on the other side of an outdated habit is a powerful technique, and one that allows me to do my part in helping them get exactly what they want and embrace this new—and different—chapter of their lives.

THE ICE CREAM THEORY

Imagine I ask you what your favorite flavor of ice cream is, and you say, "Vanilla." What would you do if I replied that vanilla ice cream was terrible?

The answer is likely that you'd do nothing at all. My opinion wouldn't matter. You're not emotionally attached enough to vanilla ice cream to fight for its honor.

Money, on the other hand, is high stakes. It's emotional. It triggers visceral responses because often our financial status is tied tightly to our identity. If someone brings me their portfolio, and I point out everything that's wrong with it and every mistake they made, I might as well have called their baby ugly! They get defensive, start blaming, and the conversation comes to an abrupt stop. This is a mistake a lot of advisers make because they want to demonstrate their authority and prove they are the smartest person in the room.

"Here's what I know that you don't, and that's why you need me!"

In our company, we aren't the heroes, our clients are, because no one likes to feel dumb. A skilled communicator frames corrections as opportunities for clarity or shared understanding, rather than highlighting errors. Not only that, but he or she would also take on the blame. If you've read Chris Voss' book, you'll know this technique as an "accusation audit." I'll sometimes say to my clients, "You're probably going to hate me for this, and you may want to walk out of here, but there was an investment that could have been added to your portfolio that would have made you thousands of dollars last year. I'm sorry your previous adviser didn't tell you about it. Would you like me to see how we could get a similar result?"

Framing it that way, I've demonstrated expertise while at the same time opening the door to collaboration. They are less likely to argue, because I've softened their defenses. Now, it becomes *their* idea to let me lead!

STAY IN THE GAME

It might surprise you to hear that one of the most powerful methods that trained me to be a successful and effective adviser didn't come from a textbook, but from the boxing ring.

I've been boxing for years It's a great mental challenge, and one that is widely misunderstood. Audiences see it as opponent vs. opponent, but the boxers know that the toughest fight is not against each other but against themselves. The most ruthless battle is fought in their own minds. Mike Tyson once said, "Everyone has a plan 'til they get punched in the face." You learn a lot about yourself when you're getting hit in the face! Mainly, whether you have the willpower to stay in the ring. Once that bell rings, you've got to stay in. Two minutes might feel like two hours but if you can just convince yourself that "this too shall pass," you can tough it out. I know for sure that at some point it will end.

The market is no different. The one thing we can count on is that it will fluctuate. The savviest investors know this, and stay in. Others panic, pull their money out and miss out on major gains when the market inevitably rights itself.

No matter what your goal is, there will be ups and downs. There will be moments of stagnation; moments you're tempted to give up. I started this business during one of the worst recessions since the Great Depression. The first few years were terrible. The month I started, I found out my wife was pregnant with our first child. When she was born, we still had no health insurance and hardly any clients. I wasn't making nearly enough money to support a family, but I had a vision. I had a goal. I had a direction.

My grandmother came to this country by herself at just sixteen years old. The same tenacity my grandparents instilled in my father, my parents then instilled in me. In fact, our family motto is "sempre avanti," which means "always forward." It's in my DNA and is now the philosophy of my company. My goal is to ensure that my clients are always moving forward towards a better future. I think about my parents. I think about what they must have felt having worked so hard for so long only to see it all evaporate into thin air. My entry into this industry wasn't easy, but I'm glad I stayed in the ring, because now I can make sure that someone else's parents are crying tears of joy, not loss.

At the end of the day, my goal isn't just to win someone's business—it's to leave each person who walks through my door better off than when they walked in, whether they work with me or not. Every conversation is an opportunity to provide insight and help people build a vision they are excited about and a plan to make that vision a reality.

It's never about convincing my clients to invest in me, but rather inspiring them to invest in themselves, and to keep their momentum moving in one direction... *always forward.*

About Nico

Nico's journey, shaped by a family of immigrants, is a testament to the power of perseverance and tenacity. Inspired by his grandmother, who, by herself at just sixteen, braved a journey across the Atlantic to come to America from Northern Italy. The influence of his grandparents instilled in Nico an unwavering belief that everyone deserves the opportunity to pursue what matters most. This conviction was further fueled when he witnessed his retired parents struggle to safeguard their hard-earned savings during the 2008 financial crisis. Determined to make a difference, Nico founded Momentum Wealth in 2009 to ensure families like his could thrive, not just survive.

Momentum Wealth isn't just another advisory firm—they're a team known for giving clients confidence and belief in what's possible and the freedom to pursue it all. With a laser focus on building robust, adaptable retirement plans and navigating changing markets, Nico has crafted an industry-leading firm that feels as close-knit and personal as a family office. At the heart of Momentum Wealth is the belief that deep, meaningful relationships are the foundation of success. That's why Nico and his team prioritize ongoing client education and appreciation events, and involvement in the community. Their work with organizations like Make-A-Wish Utah reflects their commitment to serving beyond the financial realm.

In a sea of one-size-fits-all advice, Nico has set his firm apart by offering tailored, personalized plans and service. He understands that behind every portfolio is a person—someone with dreams, fears, and a desire to get it right. This relentless focus on the human side of financial planning has earned Momentum Wealth a reputation as a team of leaders who measure their success not just by industry metrics, but by the lives they transform.

For Nico, the ultimate reward hasn't just been growing a successful firm; its watching clients realize, once a plan is created, that everything they've sacrificed for over the past 20, 30 or 40 years was worth it by giving families the confidence to live the retirement they've earned and deserve.

Outside of work, Nico's greatest pride is his family—his incredible wife and three amazing children. Together, they embrace life to the fullest, whether traveling, exploring the outdoors, or dedicating their time to giving back. These moments of connection and purpose fuel his passion both personally and professionally, reminding him of what truly matters—helping everyone always move forward.

Learn more:

- https://retiremomentum.com
- Instagram: https://www.instagram.com/retiremomentum
- LinkedIn: https://www.linkedin.com/in/nicopesci

CHAPTER 6

SALES AS A SERVICE

By Dr. Norm Dabalos

We've all been there.

You're going about your day when it's suddenly interrupted by the shrill ringing of your phone. It's a number you don't recognize, and you're tempted to ignore it. Then, some kind of morbid curiosity compels you to answer, and you're instantly sorry you did.

First, there's the pause underscored by the unmistakable static of a call center.

"Hello?" You say again, this time with a hint of irritation.

Then the scripted voice of a telemarketer pierces the silence, peddling something you didn't ask for and don't want.

When a telemarketer calls, we expect to be annoyed. We expect to be sold to. In this case, however, that sales call changed the trajectory of my entire life.

I was an engineering student at the time. I had recently been injured and was in excruciating pain every day. I had tried massage, stretching and exercising but nothing was helping. A doctor told me I had two options: Learn to live with the pain or have a complicated surgery and risk losing the use of my legs. I wasn't happy with either of those.

So that day when the telemarketer asked if I would like to take advantage of a local promotion and visit a chiropractor, I had nothing to lose and said yes. My desire to have my problem solved outweighed any trepidation I might have had accepting the promotion.

I went to the chiropractor and after a few sessions, my pain was gone. I was so grateful and moved by the experience that I ultimately left engineering and became a chiropractor. Today I run a thriving chiropractic practice in Hawaii and my mission is to deliver treatment plans that help my patients get their lives back.

So even though I can say that a telemarketing call changed my life—it's because their message matched my needs and desires.

The next time a telemarketer calls you, you may want to hear them out.

What School Doesn't Teach You

Early in my chiropractic career I had a patient who fundamentally changed the way I viewed my role as a chiropractor. He was a middle-aged man, athletic build, who had suffered from chronic back pain for years. Like many people, he had tried everything—physical therapy, medication, even surgery—but nothing seemed to work. He was skeptical, to say the least, about chiropractic care. I remember his words distinctly during the initial consultation: "I don't think this is going to help, but I'm out of options."

I was confident in my skills. I'd been trained by some of the best in the field, and I knew my adjustments could bring relief. I began the treatment and, as I expected, the results were almost immediate. His posture improved, and he left the clinic walking a little straighter. Yet something happened that I didn't anticipate. Despite the visible improvements, he didn't return. A few weeks later, I followed up, asking how he was feeling and why he hadn't booked any more sessions.

"I don't know," he said, "I felt a little better after the adjustment, but I'm still not sure this is what I need. I don't see how a few cracks here and there can solve what's been a problem for years."

This was my first wake-up call. It wasn't that I hadn't performed the adjustment correctly. It wasn't that I lacked technical skill. It was something else. I realized then that the real challenge wasn't just in delivering an adjustment; it was in convincing patients to trust the process—to see beyond the immediate relief and embrace long-term care. The problem wasn't just in their bodies; it was in their minds. And, as it turns out, in mine as well.

When I reflect on my time in chiropractic school, it's easy to remember the rigorous hours spent perfecting my technique. I prided myself on mastering the art of adjusting. As a former engineer I naturally gravitated to the Gonstead technique which is an engineering approach to the spine. My analytical mind found it fascinating.

I was one of the top students in my class, and had every reason to believe that my technical proficiency would lead to a successful career. At least that's what my professors told me. I studied hard, practiced diligently, attended seminars and shadowed countless doctors in the field.

However, chiropractic school, like many academic institutions, is focused on the technical aspect of chiropractic. The curriculum is heavily weighted towards anatomy, physiology, and biomechanics - all subjects needed to pass the national board exams. I learned how to assess a patient's physical condition, identify problems, and administer adjustments to correct spinal misalignments. What I didn't learn was how to communicate effectively with patients or help them understand the value of what I was offering.

It wasn't until I started my own practice that I realized I'd been trained to treat the body, but not to manage a business, or how to have strategic conversations that could sell what I was offering as a solution.

When I first opened the doors to my own chiropractic practice, I was filled with excitement and optimism. I had worked so hard to get to this point, and finally had the opportunity to make my mark in the healthcare world; my own clinic—a space where I could apply everything I had learned and bring relief to people in pain. I envisioned patients pouring in, eager for my expertise.

I had the equipment, the office, the skills, and a passion for helping people. I was told (and believed) that would be enough. I thought that once people experienced my adjustments, they would immediately understand the benefits, tell their friends and family, and keep coming back for more.

But as the days turned into weeks and the weeks into months, I noticed something strange. While some patients would come for one or two visits, many wouldn't return for follow-ups. It puzzled me. I knew my adjustments were working, and I had the evidence. Yet, my patient base wasn't growing. I wasn't building the kind of long-term relationships with people that I expected.

It became painfully clear that technical skill wasn't enough. The reality check hit me hard—running a successful practice involved much more than just being a good doctor.

The biggest challenge I faced wasn't getting patients into the door; it was getting them to stay. I realized I wasn't communicating the value of chiropractic care effectively. I wasn't explaining the process in a way that made sense to them, in a way that addressed their doubts and skepticism. I knew that chiropractic care could alleviate their pain, but they didn't see the long-term benefit. For many, it was just a temporary fix, and I hadn't done enough to show them the bigger picture.

I remember countless conversations where I felt like I was speaking an entirely different language from my patients. I'd talk about subluxations and spinal alignment, while they'd ask questions like, "But will this fix my pain permanently?" I was so focused on the technical side of things that I forgot to meet my patients where they were—emotionally and mentally.

I started to understand that my problem wasn't a lack of skill, it was communication. I needed to learn how to talk to my patients in a way that helped them see the value of chiropractic care, not just as a short-term solution but as a long-term investment in their health.

I had to go beyond delivering a great adjustment.

This was a major shift. Up until this point, I had believed that results would speak for themselves. But results only mattered if patients stayed long enough to experience them. And that was where I was failing.

At my breaking point, frustrated and disillusioned, I decided to hire business coaches.

My coaches didn't waste time pointing out the flaws in my approach. They helped me see that my beliefs about sales and business were deeply limiting my practice. I had viewed "sales" as a dirty word—something that didn't belong in healthcare. I thought my only job was to heal, and that business would naturally follow. But as my coaches explained, this mindset was preventing me from growing.

I had been taught to focus solely on being a great doctor, but that left me ill-prepared to run a successful business. My coaches helped me understand that sales and communication are not separate from healthcare; they are a vital part of it.

Unfortunately, most of the coaching companies I had tried were locked into old ways of doing things. While they helped me understand the basics of business, their approach to sales was extremely outdated. Approaches that may have worked 40 or 50 years ago, quite frankly, push patients away in today's market.

I began to unravel this thing called sales. I started to see that selling wasn't something you do to people—it was something you do for them. I had to let go of my belief that patients would automatically see the value in what I was offering. I had to communicate that value in a way that made sense to them.

I realized that my job as a chiropractor wasn't just to deliver great adjustments. It was also to guide my patients through the decision-making process, helping them see how chiropractic care could improve their lives. This meant explaining the benefits clearly, addressing their fears and doubts, and showing them the path forward.

This shift in mindset was transformative. I no longer saw sales as something to be avoided or ashamed of. Instead, I embraced it as an essential part of serving my patients.

GOOD BUSINESS IS PERSONAL

The note was scrawled in the sweet, crooked, swirly handwriting of a ten-year-old girl.

"Thank you for helping my mom."

Her mom, Jessica, had called my office after years of suffering from fibromyalgia. She was so sensitive and her pain so intense that she couldn't stand to be touched. She hadn't hugged her daughter in years. She had visited medical doctors whose prescriptions only numbed the pain temporarily, but it always came back. My job was to find out why. If her symptom was pain upon touch, the answer wasn't to treat the pain, but to go deeper and treat the cause of it. Imagine you buy a new toaster and it's not working properly. A lot of doctors would tell you to buy a new one. Not me. I'm going to check the plug, check the circuit breaker, and find out why this brand-new toaster isn't working. In Jessica's case, her nervous system was incredibly overstimulated. I needed to relieve the pressure on her nerves. This would require me to touch her.

Imagine the amount of trust I had to build to persuade her to allow me to do that when every touch would initially be excruciating.

I had to tune into what she really wanted. Common sense might say she wanted to get rid of the pain, but her true "why" was much deeper than that. She wanted to hug her child. No matter who you're negotiating with, you've got to be willing to go deep. Ninety percent of the time people are looking for a practical solution to an emotional problem. If I had spewed a bunch of industry jargon and explained nerve innervation of the anatomy of the interverterbral disc, I would have lost her. Instead, I explained how our work together would allow her to hold her little girl. A few treatments would allow her to be the mother she wanted to be. It worked. And a few weeks later, her daughter brought me that thank you note. I still have it to this day and keep it as a reminder that sales is a service.

Years ago, things were different. The man or woman in the

white coat knew best and patients dutifully followed their advice. Today, expectations have changed. This is true in every business from retail to banking to technology. Emotional intelligence is now both a currency and a requirement.

You've got to be willing to invest the time, ask questions, and take on the persona of a persistent child who repeatedly asks why.

"What brings you into my office today?"

"I want to get out of pain."

"Why?"

"Because the pain is affecting my life."

"Why?"

"I can't even golf or play with my kids."

(There it is.) "What if I told you that our work together could improve your golf game and allow you to be the dad you want to be—would that be worth it?"

"Yes!"

Yes, building trust and getting to the meat of the other person's desire takes time. But as Seth Godin wrote in The Purple Cow, "If you don't have time to do it right, what makes you think you'll have time to do it over?"

WHATEVER YOU ARE, YOU'RE A HUMAN FIRST

One of the most important lessons I learned during this journey was that sales is not about pushing people into something they don't need. It's about helping them make the best decision for their health. This was a radical shift in how I viewed my role as a chiropractor.

Instead of avoiding sales, I started to embrace it as a service I was providing to my patients. I wasn't just adjusting their spines; I was helping them make choices that would improve their quality of life. I learned to present chiropractic care as an investment in their future, not just a quick fix for their pain.

This new perspective changed everything. I no longer felt uncomfortable talking to patients about the benefits of long-term care. I saw it as my duty to educate them, to guide them toward making decisions that would help them live healthier, happier lives.

Ultimately, my entire approach to chiropractic care transformed when I reframed sales as something I did for my patients, not to them. It wasn't about convincing them to buy something; it was about helping them understand the value of investing in their health. Once I made this shift, I became more confident in my ability to serve my patients.

I learned that selling chiropractic care was not about manipulation or pressure. It was about guiding patients toward the best possible solution for their health concerns. By doing so, I became not just a better chiropractor but also a better communicator, educator, and advocate for my patients' well-being.

This transformation wasn't easy, but it was necessary. It allowed me to finally build the thriving practice I'd always envisioned. I am now proudly a chiropractor *and* a salesman *and* a closer for chiropractic.

When I show up like that, ready to lead, guide, and serve, spines aren't the only things that come beautifully into balance.

About Dr. Norm

Dr. Norm was born, raised, and currently lives in the city of Kailua on the island of Oahu in the state of Hawaii. Growing up in the islands, he's always had an active lifestyle. He played, coached, and refereed soccer and was very active in the performing arts. He proudly says, "I'm a Bright kid," having done theater under the direction of educator Ron Bright in the '80s and '90s. He's also served on the Board of Directors for the I'm A Bright Kid Foundation, which supports the performing arts and education.

He still enjoys performing and has been seen on *Hawaii 5-0* a few times and still does community theater. He continues to sing professionally several times per month and had the honor of being selected by Grammy winner Regina Belle to sing with her at the Blue Note in Waikiki.

He attended the University of Hawaii at Manoa then moved to the mainland, ultimately graduating with honors from Arizona State University with his degree in engineering. He worked as an engineer in Charlotte, NC for a few years then went back to school at Life University earning his Doctor of Chiropractic, magna cum laude.

In over twenty years of chiropractic practice, he's served on chiropractic mission trips to El Salvador and Guatemala. He was also selected to be the backstage chiropractor for various performers including Aerosmith, KISS, The Eagles, John Mayer, and Carrie Underwood. He is a former personal trainer and fitness instructor and was the senior trainer for North America with Les Mills International where he trained fitness instructors in kickboxing, weightlifting, and Latin and hip-hop dance.

His first exposure to chiropractic was when he injured himself during a dance performance, finally finding success with chiropractic. It has since become his mission to educate people about chiropractic, so they can make educated decisions about their own health.

His commitment to education continues. He has served as an adjunct professor at his alma mater, Life University in Atlanta, he currently hosts the *Chiro Compass* podcast for chiropractic students, and now teaches sales training for chiropractors with the premier sales trainers in the industry: CloseForChiro.

To learn more, visit hawaiigonsteadchiro.com.

CHAPTER 7

THE INEVITABLE REWARDS OF TAKING A RISK

By Oscar Diaz

I was eight years old when I first saw it—the sleek, beige box with the glowing screen.

It was a Macintosh computer, and I'd never seen anything like it before. It felt like a doorway into a world I'd only imagined through the pages of science-fiction books. With this machine I could explore places far beyond what I knew and bring my ideas to life. It felt as if the future was opening up right in front of me, and I had to be part of it.

I was captivated!

But then my parents said the words that broke the spell: "We can't afford it." In an instant the world that had just expanded in my mind was shut down. We always had enough growing up—enough to get by, enough to feel secure—but we had enough because there were always limits and restrictions. And from that moment, I made up my mind: I would do whatever it took to always have *more* than enough.

I didn't have my own computer until a decade later at university. That hunger for technology and the opportunity it represented never left me. It only grew stronger. After college I got a job with a big telecommunications company and was earning a great income. Life seemed stable, and I had a family of my own. But stability is fragile, and by 2011, Venezuela, my home, was unraveling into political unrest and economic collapse. It was no longer safe to live there.

I packed up my family and moved to Canada. It was a bold move, but a necessary one. I started working as a contractor but was then offered a job with a large oil and gas company that came with a life-changing compensation package. It was security handed to us on a silver platter. I had to decide: take a chance and go the entrepreneurial route, or go back to the corporate world.

I couldn't help wondering, "What if I didn't accept this offer? What if I opened my own business, became my own boss, and did things my own way? What if this move was a nudge to make that leap?"

I thought of my dad, who had always wanted to own his own business but felt that his responsibilities to the family came first. Never taking that chance was a regret that weighed on him. Now, here I was, on the brink of a new chapter and standing at a crossroads. One path held job security and a predictable income. The other path was ripe with uncertainty but with the promise of freedom.

I knew which way my heart was leaning, but I also knew that I needed the buy-in of my number one stakeholder: my wife!

A decision like this could not be taken lightly. Like any situation involving risk, uncertainty, and various potential outcomes, it called for a strategic conversation. We had to get clear on what we were dealing with and assess our options so we could move forward with confidence. After all, this would have a tremendous impact on our family, one way or the other.

It would be a big investment of time and money with no guarantee of an ROI. However, if it worked, we could have the life we dreamed of on our own terms.

We weighed the pros and cons. We talked about what we could do with the income from the corporate job and after an hour of deep negotiations, we came to a conclusion.

We took the leap of faith to fulfill my childhood dream and

founded Tecbound Technology, a full-service technology company offering IT services and comprehensive cyber security initiatives.

It was a lesson in faith and an exercise in perseverance.

More than anything, it was a challenge to develop a healthy and ongoing relationship with the one thing every visionary must get comfortable with—*risk*, and the negotiation process that goes with it.

No Risk, No Reward

Strategic conversations happen every day in both life and business. They're important because they bring clarity to complex situations, allowing you to align your actions with your long-term goals. Every moment of growth, whether personal or professional, is powered by these kinds of conversations, as they help steer us in the right direction. Conversations like these are almost always initiated when something is at stake. With higher stakes, of course, comes a greater risk.

There's no avoiding it. The key is to confront the risk while weighing the value of the potential benefits. It's an exercise I was all too familiar with and about to practice again.

You see, some say that until you make a million dollars in topline revenue, you don't have a business, you have a hobby.

I don't know if that's true or not, but it stuck with me, so hitting the million-dollar mark was my goal. Yet I had hit a plateau that I couldn't transcend. I vividly remember sitting on the couch watching YouTube when I came across an advertisement for a company that helped MSPs like me market and scale their businesses. I set up a call with them. It sounded great, but it was a $30,000 investment. I explained to my wife that this company could help us break the plateau, but if we made the investment, the new floors she wanted would have to wait.

It was time for another conversation.

A key part of any strategic conversation is the careful weighing of pros and cons, balancing the potential risks against the rewards.

It's about anticipating what could go wrong, *and* what could go exceptionally right.

Ultimately my wife generously gave up her new floors so we could invest with this company and luckily, it worked!

We are now one of the leading technology providers for First Nation Police Agencies in Canada. You see, police forces here must submit requirements every two years to comply with the Royal Canadian Mounted Police IT policies called NCACR, and many of them constantly struggle with that. We help them to be up to date on the requirements so that they are compliant and protected and we are the only company in western Canada that dedicates itself to this.

Yet even though they *need* our services, many organizations are still hesitant to make the investment. I find that the same risk-to-reward conversations I have at home are necessary during client meetings too.

I know that cyber security measures aren't cheap, but they save my clients potentially millions of dollars in lost revenue. It's my job to help them see that and to visualize what they stand to lose.

If I can't strategically communicate the value of what we do in such a way that it outweighs the perceived risk of investment, I don't make money, and they could lose everything!

I'm Latin American, and we tend to be direct. There is an inherent risk to full transparency, and I walk that line every day.

A while back I had a customer who was very budget conscious. They asked me if the cost of technology would keep going up. I said, "Yes." There was no way around it. With each technological innovation comes an increase in cost. They kept pushing and said they felt like every time they talked to me, I was pitching something.

Now of course I knew that the reason for that was due to the rapid emergence of new and more sophisticated threats to security, but they didn't see it that way. I had to change my strategy.

I sat down with them and explained what they would potentially lose if they were a victim of a security breach. I painted a picture of the consequences of ignoring my suggestions. It wasn't sales, but rather education and delivered in a spirit of service. If I didn't make the suggestions I was making, I wouldn't be doing my job, and they would be left vulnerable.

I redirected the conversation to what they could lose so that their focus could shift from the cost to the *value*.

In any negotiation, business or personal, if you can lead the other party to desire the value more than they fear the cost, you'll be well on your way to a win/win scenario.

THE VALUE OF BEING BOLD

Being bold and direct in a conversation can feel like walking a tightrope. There's always the risk of pushing too hard or making someone uncomfortable. However, I've found that the risk is worth taking because honesty fosters clarity.

When we're direct, we're not just saving time, we're building trust. Courageous honesty is refreshing in a world that seems to be overrun with inauthentic methods of persuasion.

That said, there is a risk to transparent communication and that's why so many companies and business leaders avoid it. I see too many MSPs operating from the notion that "the customer is always right." This phrase was coined to emphasize the importance of customer service, but the reality is that sometimes the customer is at worst, wrong, and at best, uninformed. In that case, following the lead of the customer could not only get you fired, it could get you sued!

I once got a phone call from a company who was unhappy with their IT vendor. After they explained the arrangement they had with this vendor, I looked through their security stack and showed them all the gateways that were still vulnerable to attack. It was clear that *they* had dictated the security plan and the guy they hired had followed it. That might sound like good customer service, but it's bad business. That vendor likely noticed that their proposed plan wouldn't be nearly comprehensive enough, yet because he wanted their business, he kept quiet, avoided a potentially triggering conversation and followed their lead.

The problem was he was following them right into an eventual security breach. Tough conversations are a part of strong leadership. Yes, occasionally I bump into a customer who takes my directness as criticism rather than expertise, but that's a risk I'm willing to take. Most of the time, a direct conversation is met with gratitude.

In the end a confident communicator establishes trust. And trust is the cornerstone of any strategic conversation, and the currency of any profitable business.

THE INVISIBLE TOOL THAT LEADS TO SUCCESS

When we think about the elements of a conversation, we think of words, tone and body language. Those things are important, but there's another element of strategic conversations that is often left unchecked, and that is the art of *persistence*.

I'm an ardent believer in stoicism and stoic philosopher Epictetus once said, "Two words should be committed to memory and obeyed by alternatively exhorting and restraining ourselves, words that will ensure we lead a mainly blameless and untroubled life."

He was referring to the words "persist and resist."

Whether I'm engaged in a conversation with my family or a client, it's my mission to persist despite any obstacles, naysayers or distractions. I am focused on our collective goals, and therefore undeterred when things become challenging.

Whether it's a hacker who gets in despite my best efforts or a negotiation that is going sideways, undesired things will happen. I cannot control that. What I can control is my level of commitment. As I write this, there are tens of thousands of IT companies in Canada all vying for the attention of the same clients. We have similar services and similar price points so it's up to me to figure out a way to stand out. While I do make sure that my marketing is up to snuff, my biggest competitive edge isn't fancy branding and a mascot. I stand out by doing the one thing that so many companies are unwilling to do: persist.

I keep calling, keep emailing and continue to follow up and offer value. My intention is to prevent them from losing everything they've worked so hard to build.

Sometimes the most important part of a strategic conversation is persistence, because real breakthroughs often come after digging deeper, pushing past initial challenges, and staying committed to finding a solution when things seem to be at a stalemate.

Sometimes the door isn't locked, it's just stuck. Most people will stop there. They'll push once and give up. That's when it pays to stay the course.

No Going Back

When I was a kid, my dad always encouraged me to read. "Read everything you can." he would say, "Reading is how you learn to form your own philosophies and opinions."

I took that advice to heart and became an avid reader, and I often bring what I learn into conversations with my clients. Not long ago a client was expressing frustration with an issue that was not IT related. He was changing his business model and having trouble getting his team to relinquish the old way of doing things. He asked what I would do, and I recalled something I had read. I told him I would probably follow the lead of Alexander the Great. When Alexander the Great reached Persia, he told his men to burn the ships so that no matter what happened, they would not be able to go back. He appreciated that advice and it occurred to me that I had spent my life burning the ships and consistently moving forward.

There is risk in that, but the possibility of great reward is inherent to every risk.

Since making the leap to start my own company, we have

expanded from serving clients in Calgary to also serving clients in Latin America and have grown 200 percent in the last three years.

Taking risks and having courageous strategic conversations isn't just a choice—it's a necessity. Waiting for the perfect time or the right moment often means waiting forever. In business, as in life, you have to be willing to act, even when the outcome is uncertain. My father's advice to "read everything you can" taught me that learning is how we form our philosophies, but *action* is how we put those philosophies to the test.

Starting my own company was a leap into the unknown, but burning those corporate ships allowed me to push forward without looking back.

None of this would've happened if I had shied away from tough conversations and waited for the perfect moment. The real secret to success is that the perfect moment comes when you decide to create it.

About Oscar

Oscar Diaz has twenty years of experience in the IT industry. Oscar studied Information Technology Engineering at UNITEC (http://www.unitec.edu.ve/). During his five-year program, he worked as a Coding Instructor and participated in several university programs to attract new students to the faculty. After graduating, Oscar started working in the telecommunications industry at Digitel Corp (www.digitel.com.ve). His first position at Digitel was as a System Administrator, where he had several servers under his responsibility, including the email system that supported three thousand users. In the next five years, Oscar demonstrated he was willing to take on new challenges and responsibilities; this allowed him to climb the organizational ladder and earn a management position where he was in charge of the server infrastructure running on Microsoft products (two hundred-plus servers and ten-plus engineers on his team under his direction).

After that, Oscar moved to the position of Application Manager, where he oversaw (a) Business Intelligence, (b) Web Application Development, and (c) Customer Liaison Units (where he had twenty-plus engineers, business analysts and team leads working under his supervision). After ten years working in the Enterprise world and seeing the opportunity of bringing Enterprise IT practices to small and medium- sized businesses, Oscar founded Tecbound Technology in 2011. The goal of the company was to bring quality IT service to business owners and help them navigate the challenges of using IT in their business. Tecbound has grown ever since and now has a presence in Calgary, Vancouver, and Latin America.

Oscar sponsors several children through not-for-profit organizations like World Vision and Christians Children's Fund, and has a passion for helping kids to get involved in sports activities to promote family values, respect for others and encourage them to become the best they can be.

CHAPTER 8

BREAKFAST WITH LARRY KING

Conversations on the Edge of Chaos

By Nick Nanton

"The clock hit 0:00...Sold!"

The charity auction site just stared back at me. It was a bit surreal—no applause, no fanfare, just me by myself in my office at my computer. I had just bid on and won a private breakfast with Larry King.

Yes, *the* Larry King.

My heart was racing, partly because I had just spent more than I ever had on a charity auction item, and partly because I had scored the chance to have a sit-down conversation with one of the most legendary media personalities in the world and a personal hero of mine.

My entire company is powered by conversations of all kinds.

I initiate conversations with people whose stories I hope to tell. I lead conversations with my team on how we can fulfill our mission of "helping the right people help more people." And I seek out conversations with visionaries I admire and hope to have the opportunity to learn from. In fact, I was inspired to start producing documentaries because when I first started my career, I was on a quest to grow personally and professionally but I couldn't even afford a ticket to a Tony Robbins seminar. I figured if I could make films that told important stories and answered important questions, other people, including young professionals, inspired teenagers, or even just people looking for the next chapter in life, could watch them online with little to no cost barrier. I had no idea that spark of inspiration would grow into DNA Films® and expand into a world-class production team, but I'm grateful that it did. Since then, I've had a few full-circle moments in which I am now the one that people are calling for advice or inviting to speak in college classrooms. That's a humbling experience! I'm always willing to find time in my calendar for people who are truly interested in learning, but what I've found is that they often don't have the experience to even know what to ask.

I'd get on the phone with them and be met with radio silence. I can't help thinking how much more I could give them if they had a more solid idea of what they hoped to get out of meeting me, if we could engage in an intentionally strategic conversation that delivered guidance and sparked new ideas rather than engaging in awkward chitchat. I was determined not to make that same mistake with Larry King.

Sometimes the key is preparation. Sometimes it's flexibility. Often it's the sweet spot in between.

TEETERING ON THE EDGE OF CHAOS

Most of the success I've enjoyed can be traced back to a series of conversations. They were strategic in the sense that they were initiated with a purpose in mind, but a *flexible* one.

The "edge of chaos" is a concept from systems theory, and it resides in the sweet spot between total order and complete chaos. Imagine you're trying to run a business, or even just manage your day-to-day life. If everything is super rigid, following the same exact routine or rules, there's no room for creativity, for growth, or even to pivot when the unexpected happens. You're stuck in a controlled, predictable zone. On the flip side, if there's too much randomness or chaos, it's incredibly inefficient and often little to nothing gets done.

The edge of chaos might sound ominous, but it's actually where

BREAKFAST WITH LARRY KING

innovation can thrive. You're organized enough to be prepared, but flexible enough to adapt if necessary.

In a practical sense, operating on the edge of chaos means you're constantly pushing boundaries and staying flexible, but grounded enough to maintain alignment.

When I had the chance to eat breakfast with Larry King, I knew it was a once-in-a-lifetime experience. I had admired him for years and was grateful just to meet him, but I also knew it was my one chance to maybe work with one of the most iconic journalists of all time.

I knew I had to strike a balance between being strategic and being authentic. I had to stay grounded in the moment while remaining open to what might be possible. Essentially, I needed to eat breakfast on the edge of chaos!

The question I try to walk into any meeting with is "Where could this lead?" Not where *should* it lead, which immediately restricts the possibilities, but where *could* it lead?

When the day of the breakfast arrived, I was excited but unattached to any outcome. If nothing else, I'd walk away with a great story. I drove to the deli in Beverly Hills, and not long after, Larry King walked in. He told me that he appreciated my donation and said the magic words: "How can I help you?" The reality is, he didn't have to help me at all. His obligation was simply to show up and eat some toast. I would come to learn, however, that Larry was a very generous person, and I was careful not to take advantage of that. I told him I had just three questions. I said, "One, I want to do more interviews, and you've done more interviews than anyone in the world, so I'd like to learn from you. Two, I bet you have some incredible stories, and I'd love to hear them. Three, I would love to work with you in some way, but you don't know me yet, so I just want to park that thought in the back of your brain for now."

He gave me a few fantastic tips, including to go right for what is the most obviously uncomfortable topic. He told me that if someone had a big bruise on their face, that would be the first thing he'd ask about. Larry was brilliant, and at the end of the breakfast I said to him, "How come nobody has told your story?" To which he shrugged.

"I would love the opportunity to explore that," I said, "but you have never seen anything I've done. Could I send you a recent documentary I did about Peter Diamandis?"

"Sure," he said. "Then call me. Here's my number."

I sent him the film and followed up with a phone call a few weeks later. He said he enjoyed it, but I would need to speak to his agent, as they had already promised the rights to his story to a friend of his. His agent told me he'd find out if Larry's friend would partner with me. I was at Notre Dame filming a documentary on the legendary Rudy Ruettiger when I got the phone call.

It was a no.

I wasn't giving up. I called Larry on the number he'd given me and asked if he would be a guest on my internet TV show. He said yes. The only problem was, I didn't actually have an internet TV show. So overnight I created one called *In Case You Didn't Know with Nick Nanton*, and Larry King was my first guest. You can watch it all on Amazon Prime.

That interview was ninety minutes of mind-blowing stories and insights, and I knew I had a hit. I took it to my editor and asked him to turn the interview into a documentary. The result was a beautiful piece that walked the viewer through the epic life of a legend. I then had to give Larry a heads-up. After all, we had discussed him being on my internet TV show, and I had been told that I couldn't do his documentary. I explained that I was really excited with what my team had put together, but it was a little different than originally discussed and asked to show it to him. He invited me to come to his house. I booked a flight for the next week, and before long I was sitting in his living room, which was decorated with Emmy Awards and pictures with nearly every celebrity one could think of, and I won't lie, I had an emotional moment. Here I was, an immigrant kid from Barbados sitting in Larry King's house in Beverly Hills. When the screening was over, my heart was beating so fast, and I'm pretty sure there was sweat dripping down my forehead. He turned to me and said, "Excellent work. Now what do we do with it?"

This was my moment. This was the edge. I said, "How about I make more of these. I'll do all the work, you be an executive producer, put me in touch with some of your friends and keep one-third of whatever we make."

"Done," he said. I was so nervous I almost didn't hear him! What had just happened? I was doing backflips inside I was so excited!

What started as a charity breakfast ended with Larry King as my business partner. We made an entire season of that show and won an Emmy together, and shortly after that he passed away.

I'm pretty sure none of that would have happened had I walked into that breakfast with rigid expectations and a sense of entitlement.

Sometimes the edge of chaos, while uncomfortable, becomes the birthplace of collaboration, creativity, and a life-changing friendship.

MEDIA AS A CATALYST FOR CONVERSATION

Years ago I had the pleasure of interviewing Nido Qubein, president of High Point University. He told the story of the time he delivered a keynote for a company and afterward was approached by the CEO. The company was looking for a consultant, and the CEO asked Nido if he knew anyone who might be a fit. And he did—himself! The problem was that he wasn't positioned as a business consultant but rather as a speaker. So, he wrote a book.

He made sure that book demonstrated his business expertise, sent it to the CEO, and landed the seven-figure consulting gig himself.

When I was hoping to get Larry King to let me tell his story, I knew I needed to position myself as a powerful storyteller. So, I sent him documentaries I had already directed and produced.

A strategic conversation isn't limited to words. Media can play a big part in an ongoing conversation. Sending someone a book or a video is an effective way to begin a conversation because you're inviting them to explore a certain point of view, hopefully sparking their interest and opening the door for collaboration to take place.

The root word of *media* is *medi*, which means "middle." We refer to books and TV as media because they are *mediums* that are in the *middle* of newsworthy and impactful conversations. They exist as *mediators* between audiences and the information we hope will reach them, speak to them, and move them into action.

Take a **book**, for instance. It's not just a collection of words; it's a slow-burn conversation between the reader and the author. That author spent years marinating in research, synthesizing ideas, and pouring it all out for me to absorb it and be moved by it.

Now, a **documentary**? That's a whole different beast. It's a high-speed, visual assault on your senses. It doesn't ask for permission to blow your mind. In ninety minutes or less, a good documentary grabs you by the collar and shoves real people's stories, hard data, and jaw-dropping visuals into your face. It's like having a conversation with a passionate friend whose passion draws you in.

When I send a book to someone, I'm inviting them to a conversation already in progress in the hope that they'll join.

Different forms of media are like secret weapons in the arsenal of strategic conversations. Each one—whether it's a book, documentary, podcast, or even social media post—is a bridge that transforms fleeting interest into meaningful, strategic conversations—conversations that can lead to collaboration, opportunity, and, ultimately, impact.

THE GIFT THAT KEEPS ON GIVING

In 2018 I directed a documentary called *Rudy Ruettiger: The Walk On*, which explored the real life of Daniel "Rudy" Ruettiger, the inspiration behind the iconic sports film *Rudy*. I mentioned it before, because I remember being there on set when I got the fateful call telling me I couldn't make Larry's documentary.

One day Rudy told me he'd like me to interview legendary sports anchor Dick Vitale for his documentary. I reached out to Dick, and he kindly agreed. We set a date for me to visit his home to interview him. Dick, known to most as Dickie V, is a fascinating guy who had enjoyed a wildly successful career in the sports industry. I was there to tell Rudy's story, but I couldn't help wondering, "Why hadn't anyone told Dick Vitale's story yet?"

So, I asked him the same question I asked Larry King: "Why hasn't anyone told your story?" Just like Larry, he shrugged. You can guess my next question, and what I did over the next few months to gain his trust in my storytelling ability mirrored what I had done with Larry. Eventually, Dick agreed to let me tell his story. We began a two-year project that started with multiple rejections by major networks and ended with a dynamic film that I am extremely proud of called *Dickie V*. We eventually sold it to Disney and ESPN.

That kind of result requires a not-so-secret ingredient that turns a regular conversation into a *strategic, purposeful* one: persistence.

Persistence is the muscle that keeps a conversation moving forward. In a strategic conversation, you're not just exchanging pleasantries; you're driving toward a goal—whether it's closing a deal, making a decision, or setting the course for your next big move. And that rarely happens in one tidy, thirty-minute chat. It's messy, frustrating, and full of moments where you'll feel like throwing in the towel. That's where persistence kicks in. Persistence keeps you coming back to the table, even when you hit roadblocks. It's about not taking no for an answer until you've exhausted all the possibilities, found the blind spots, and dug deep enough to get to the real issue.

Without persistence tough conversations fizzle out before they can produce anything meaningful. People retreat into their comfort zones, and the bold strategies that could change the game never see the light of day. But with persistence, you push past the initial resistance and keep the conversation alive until you reach clarity, alignment, and action.

The definition of a conversation is a talk between two or more people. You've got to have your sights set on how the conversation affects others, what they can contribute, and how they might respond. There is a give-and-take that is dependent on the exchange of time and the mutual commitment to listening.

Notice I didn't say agreeing, but rather *listening.*

And if you listen closely enough and stay curious, you'll find that there is always another step you can take, another idea to bring to life, and another fascinating story to tell.

About Nick

From the slums of Port-au-Prince, Haiti, with special forces raiding a sex trafficking ring and freeing children, to the Virgin Galactic Space Port in Mojave with Sir Richard Branson, twenty-two-time Emmy Award–winning Director-Producer Nick Nanton has become known for telling stories that connect. Why? Because he focuses on the most fascinating subject in the world: *people*. As an award-winning songwriter, storyteller, and best-selling author, Nick has shared his message with millions of people through his documentaries, speeches, blogs, lectures, songs, and best-selling books. Nick's book *StorySelling* hit The Wall Street Journal Best-Seller List and is available on Audible as an audiobook. Nick has directed more than sixty documentaries and a sold-out Broadway Show (garnering forty-three Emmy nominations in multiple regions and twenty-two wins), including:

- *DICKIE V* (ESPN/Disney+)
- *Rudy Ruettiger: The Walk On* (Amazon Prime)
- *The Rebound* (Netflix)
- *Operation Toussaint* (Amazon Prime)

Nick has shared the stage with, coauthored books with, and made films featuring:

- Larry King
- Kathie Lee Gifford
- Hoda Kotb
- Dick Vitale
- Kenny Chesney
- Magic Johnson
- Coach Mike Krzyzewski
- Jack Nicklaus
- Tony Robbins
- Lisa Nichols
- Peter Diamandis
- And many more

Nick specializes in bringing the element of human connection to every viewer, no matter the subject. He is currently directing and hosting the series *In Case You Didn't Know* (season 1 executive produced by Larry King), featuring legends in the worlds of business, entrepreneurship, personal development, technology, and sports.

Nick's first love has always been music. He has been writing songs for more than two decades, and his songs have been aired on radio across the

United States and in Canada. He is currently ranked in the top 10 percent of songwriters in the world. His songs have been recorded by Lee Brice, Darius Rucker, RaeLynn, Joe Bryson, and many more, and have amassed more than three million streams on Spotify, Apple Music, Pandora, and SoundCloud. He received three Gold records in 2018 for his work with the global touring band A Day to Remember.

Nick has written and/or produced songs that have appeared on the following shows or in promotional commercials for:

- the Fox prime-time series *Glee*, *New Girl*, *House*, and *Hell's Kitchen*
- the MLB All-Star Game
- ABC Family's hit series *Falcon Beach*
- the CBS prime-time series *Ghost Whisperer* starring Jennifer Love Hewitt

CHAPTER 9

CONVERSATIONS THAT COUNT

The Art of Strategic Mentorship

By James P. Engel

The weathered trailers lined what felt like a forgotten patch of land framed in gravel and dust.

Faded clothes hung from lines stretched across make-shift porches, and the air was thick with disappointment, the atmosphere framed by rows of American dreams gone wrong. My family was loving and hardworking, but dreams could only stretch as far as the money, and there wasn't much of it.

For a lot of the community, success was measured by the ability to make it to the next month without the collection agency calling. Physically, I was a child in that trailer park. Mentally, I was already planning my exit.

Growing up poor often leads to an overwhelming goal of "being rich someday," and I was no different. I appreciated what we had, but the allure of having more never quite left me alone. As soon as I could get out, I did.

Fast-forward a few years, and I went on to build a multimillion-dollar real estate company. Over the course of my career, I have been fortunate enough to close more than eight thousand real estate and mortgage transactions. It's hard even for me to believe that a kid who grew up in a five-hundred-dollar home could eventually generate enough income to retire by the age of forty, but that's what happened. Only I didn't do it alone. I recognized early in life that if

I wanted a different reality, I'd have to learn from people who were living the life I aspired to live. I read every book I could and studied the habits of the wealthiest people in the world. I loved my community. But I wanted more, and as nice as they were, I was pretty sure none of them could teach me how to be a millionaire.

If you look at what the wealthiest people in the world have in common, it isn't just money, it's mentorship. Amazon CEO Jeff Bezos was mentored by Bill Gates, who was mentored by Warren Buffet, who was mentored by Benjamin Graham. All these men became billionaires not just because they are brilliant, but because they are humble. Each of them understood the value of seeking advice from folks who were a few steps ahead. Mentorship, having one and being one, is the secret sauce to creating a lineage of wisdom and success that powers innovation, breaks new ground, and eventually, changes the world.

Premeditated Success

At a very young age I reached the pinnacle of my career at Edward Jones becoming the number one stockbroker in our division.

I invested right, bought a big house, a boat, wave runners and pretty much every toy you can think of that a young guy with too much money might have. By the age of twenty-seven, I could retire. I was a walking cliché, the young, bored millionaire. It might sound like a dream, but it's tough going from being a workaholic to having nothing to do and nowhere you needed to be. I started to seek out a new challenge.

Right around that time I took a trip to Phoenix and met with a network marketing company at a beautiful golf course. At first, I was confused. What did golf have to do with network marketing? Then the guy in charge handed me a tape to watch. The video tapes were selling membership packages. For five hundred dollars a person could join this club and get free rounds of golf and a bunch of other members-only perks. I bought three hundred videos to distribute. A whopping 95 percent of the people I gave one to took the deal and before I knew it, I was invited to fly to Salt Lake City to accept the Eagle Award, an award given to the top sales associate in the company.

They flew my wife and I out to the event in first class and a limousine transported us from the airport to the venue where eight thousand other associates were gathered. They invited me on stage and suddenly all eyes were on me. After the ceremony, everyone was asking me how I did it and I had to chuckle. I didn't know a thing about golf or network marketing. What I did know about was how to have a strategic conversation.

And I was about to have another one that would change my life...

Across the room was an older guy wearing an expensive suit with a Scottsdale Troon Golf Club Quail on the collar. He exuded wealth.

"Who's that?" I asked. The perplexed faces staring back at me told me that I should have already known.

"You don't know?" they said. "That's Tom Murphy. He owns *everything*. He created this company. He owns the golf course in Phoenix."

He was also the author of a book called Premeditated Success that would become my reference book for life. I asked for an introduction. I thanked him for the opportunity and complimented him on the extraordinary company he had created. Then I got bold and invited him to go golfing. He said yes. That was the beginning of a 30-year relationship.

We became best friends, but beyond that, Tom was my mentor. Over the years, we spent hundreds of hours in deep, strategic conversations that changed the trajectory of my life, retrained my brain and taught me how to unlock the top of my potential. That's what a good mentor does—they see the most successful version of you, before you can.

One day, I asked Tom for advice. I was running a real estate and mortgage brokerage company but had hit a plateau. I wanted more clients, and fast. Like all good mentors, he answered my question with more questions. He asked me how many clients I wanted, and

I said one hundred a month. At the time, one client translated to about $20,000. Tom made me a deal. He asked how much I would pay him if he could get me all the clients I wanted. At first, I said 10 percent. I could tell by his face it wasn't the right answer. He said, "So I'm going to do all the work and get all the clients and you're only going to give me 10 percent? I'll pass." I bumped it up to 50 percent. "So," he said, "you're willing to pay me $10,000 per customer. Great. Go out and tomorrow and spend $100,000 to get more clients."

I understood the lesson. If I was willing to give $10,000 per client to Tom, why was I hesitant to invest in growing the business? I made two thousand multimedia business cards, booked a golf course, rented the entire clubhouse for $50,000 and made it an open bar. I then invited five hundred mortgage brokers, real estate clients, and referral partners. I bought eleven hundred copies of the best success books of all time (Harv Eker's "Secrets of the Millionaire Mind") and gave everyone a copy. I hired a company to set up two screens and played the movie *The Secret* in the background. Essentially, I spent $100,000 to bring people together and create an environment that wreaked of success.

That event brought in nearly 250 new clients and more than $2.5 Million in revenue.

I'd say that $100,000 investment was well worth it. I would have never come up with that strategy on my own. At the time, I was thinking narrowly and saw only the cost of marketing, not the value. Thank goodness I had a solid mentor who saw what I couldn't see. That one conversation opened my eyes to thinking differently and investing in ways that paid off exponentially. I am beyond grateful for the conversations I've shared with Tom over the years. I found out, however, that the only thing more fulfilling than having a mentor is *being* one.

THE MENTEE BECOMES THE MENTOR

Brett was twenty-four years old when he became my client. I had never met him in person, but I knew he was a husband and father mowing lawns to make ends meet while building a real estate portfolio.

One day my assistant told me that Brett wanted to buy another home. It would be his seventh. I told her he was already over leveraged and to tell him no.

Brett was not taking no for an answer. I was swamped at the time and had 250 mortgages in the pipeline, but I told Katie to set up a meeting with him at the golf course. I intended to take one hour to set him straight but as soon as he started talking, I knew he was special. He was smart, charismatic and best of all, hungry for more. I thought about all the time Tom had given me over the years and felt compelled to pay it forward. We talked for five hours straight. I was about to launch a new real estate company I wanted this guy on my team.

I encouraged him to get his license, promised him I would feed him clients and told him I'd make him $500,000 in his first year. I created multi-media business cards for him and put him out front as the face of the brand. At the end of the first year, I didn't pay him $500,000. I had paid him closer to $1.3 million! Eventually, I was ready to retire, and I knew Brett was meant for even bigger things. I introduced him to Keller Williams Realty, and he became Gary Keller's right-hand man. When I met Brett, he was mowing lawns, cleaning pools and making less than $100,000 a year. He's now more than likely worth north of one hundred million dollars.

He just bought an entire neighborhood to build his dream estate.

When you take the time to sit in the seat of the mentor, you're not just sharing wisdom and paying it forward; you benefit too. Those conversations can unlock new perspectives and reignite your own passion for growth. Brett's success made me a lot of money! Sometimes, a simple conversation is the doorway to extraordinary possibilities—for both the mentor and the mentee.

THE RULE OF SEVEN

Over the years, I've come to realize the importance of value mirroring when it comes to strategic conversations. If my goal is to grow, then the qualities I want to cultivate in myself are the same ones I need to look for in the people I associate with. I've learned after thousands of negotiations that there are seven elements to look for in determining the quality of a connection. This system has become my benchmark for identifying those who are truly worth investing in, and it has never let me down.

1. Know versus not know

Do I know this person, and do they allow themselves to be known? A person who is transparent and authentic creates a foundation for mutual respect. People who keep their guard up or present a façade often lack the depth required for meaningful connections.

2. Like versus dislike

Do I like them? It might seem simple, but liking someone goes beyond surface-level impressions. It speaks to shared values, a sense of respect, and an ability to connect on a human level. If I don't enjoy someone's company, the likelihood of success in any other capacity is slim.

3. Trust versus not trust

Do I trust them, and do they actively seek to be trustworthy? Trust is the cornerstone of any successful relationship. If someone is trustworthy, they demonstrate consistency in their actions and intentions.

4. Giver versus taker

Is this person a giver or a taker? Givers are rare, but invaluable. They look for ways to add value without always expecting something in return. Takers, on the other hand, drain resources—time, energy, and goodwill. Surrounding yourself with givers ensures an environment of reciprocity, where everyone contributes and grows together.

5. Long-term versus short-term

Do they think in terms of long-term vision or short-term gains? Quality people approach life with a long-term mindset. They understand that success takes time, dedication, and patience. Those who focus only on short-term wins often sacrifice relationships and opportunities for quick gains.

6. Proactive versus reactive

Are they proactive or reactive? Proactive individuals take initiative and avoid being constantly caught off guard. They're the type of people who "dig their well before they're thirsty." Reactive people, on the other hand, are often in crisis mode.

7. Positive versus negative

Are they inherently positive or negative? Positivity isn't just about being cheerful on the outside—it's about core beliefs and attitudes toward life. Quality people remain solution-oriented, even when faced with setbacks. I seek out those who can stay positive as they bring energy and inspiration to every interaction.

This system has served as my compass for not only identifying quality individuals but as a reminder of the qualities I aim to embody myself.

THE MOST IMPORTANT CONVERSATION I'VE EVER HAD

Over the years, I've had the pleasure of working with and learning from people I deeply admire.

I've had the opportunity to travel widely and meet mentors whose guidance opened doors for me I couldn't have opened on my own. I've had conversations that led to millions of dollars in revenue.

I've realized, however, that the most important negotiation I ever had was with myself. My life could have gone in a drastically different direction. I recall a moment as a young boy when I somehow became aware of my surroundings and what they meant. I said to myself in that moment, "This is not all there is. I can do more, be more and have more."

That inner dialogue made me realize that success wasn't about external circumstances, but about the mindset I carried. From that day forward, I committed to nurturing that dialogue, to thinking bigger, and to seeking the wisdom of those who had already achieved what I dreamed of. Every step, every choice, every mentor and mentee interaction played a role in my evolution, and I hope I'll always keep growing.

I view my life as an ongoing negotiation between who I am and who I could become, and I pride myself in recognizing and championing the potential of others. Quite possibly the most fun and success I've had in my lifelong career pursuit in mentorship is happening currently as I transition from mentor, back to *being* mentored by one of the most inspiring and talented human beings that I have ever met.

He is one of the hardest-working, most iconic people in the business-building space—Nicholas Trevillian, Coach Nicky T. He is the founder and the CEO of The Triumphant Life Co., host of the *Triumphant Life* podcast, a show that embodies success and achieving triumph in all areas of life and has closed more than two thousand real estate transactions. I am grateful for the conversations I have with Nick.

After all, the synergy created in strategic conversations can turn potential into reality, ideas into profit, and passing strangers into lifelong friends.

About James

James P. Engel is a distinguished leader in the real estate and mortgage lending industries, boasting an impressive track record of closing over eight thousand mortgage loans and real estate transactions over nearly three decades. His extensive experience has allowed him to mentor more than two dozen multimillionaires in the field, attributing his success to the innovative systems he developed and the talented team members he has guided.

James' mission is to empower one thousand real estate agents to achieve seven-figure incomes, generating over one million dollars in gross commissions annually. He has crafted key strategic and market-dominating systems that set him apart from the competition, including:

- Revolutionary Real Estate Marketing Techniques: James employs unique marketing strategies that no one else in the industry is utilizing, such as:
  - Wow Boxes and Video Books
  - Sixteen Weekly Cialdini Letters sent to both buyers and sellers to secure their business
  - Twenty In-Depth Free Reports covering essential aspects of real estate transactions from the client's perspective
  - Engaging Monthly Newsletters designed to attract and retain clients
  - Bank Bag Mailers and a Comprehensive Database Dashboard with all marketing funnels and sequences
  - Plus, thirty-four additional innovative tools that have driven his success in closing over eight thousand transactions.

James' proven concepts for attracting new clients include:

- The Law of Large Numbers
- Prospecting on Auto-Pilot
- Active Prospecting Machines that continuously engage thousands of potential clients without requiring manual effort

- Unique value propositions that emphasize quality, quantity, and repetition
- Delivering exceptional, over-the-top value to clients

For real estate agents looking to double or triple their closings, James invites you to visit www.DominantAgent.com. This exclusive program is designed for agents and their mortgage and title partners who are serious about increasing their annual transactions.

Discover comprehensive "Done For You" real estate sales marketing solutions that you won't find anywhere else at www.DominantAgent.com.

CHAPTER 10

SUCCESS COMES IN CANS

By J ' X

"Get me a doctor."

My last words were a desperate plea as the room began to spin and I collapsed face-first into the smoky carpet of the pub. I was having lunch with my five-year-old son and his father when I felt my body betray me.

The room started spinning, and I hit the ground as muffled voices surrounded me.

"Get up," scolded his father. "You're making a scene."

But I couldn't move.

I was lifted into an ambulance, and though I was cognitively alert, I couldn't speak. I heard the paramedics say that my pulse was dropping, and I wondered how long I had until it stopped altogether. When we finally arrived at the hospital, it was like a scene from a movie. Two doctors and six nurses hoisted me onto a table and in seconds had sliced off my clothes like they were changing tires at a pit stop. I lay there exposed, my hand falling at an uncomfortable angle off the bed. I desperately wanted someone to notice and lift it up, but no one did. I couldn't communicate, couldn't move and every poke and prod sent waves of pain that contorted my body.

I was moved to ICU where I remained paralyzed for days, trapped in my own body as I listened to doctors argue over what caused my condition. I was deeply frustrated that they were talking about me as if I wasn't there and my mind was silently screaming.

Days passed in this helpless state, my mind sharp as ever, yet

I couldn't so much as whisper. One morning, I was wheeled to the bowels of the hospital for more tests. The attendant transporting me said nothing. It struck me that because they thought I couldn't hear them, they had stopped speaking to me. It was the most alone I had ever felt.

I was wheeled down a long, dark corridor, parked in front of double doors and left alone.

"Maybe this is it," I thought. "Maybe this is how it ends."

The darkness of that thought could have been my undoing but instead, a fire ignited inside me. I realized that while I couldn't move or speak, there was something I *could* do. I could *think*.

I still had the most important faculty at my disposal—my thoughts! Immediately my inner dialogue shifted from, "I don't want to die, and I don't want to be in this hallway" to everything I *did* want.

I wanted to see my son.

I wanted to see sunshine.

I wanted to walk, speak and fulfill my purpose!

I realized in that moment that I had a choice. I could accept the fate that the doctors and this burst duodenal artery were trying to pin on me, or I could choose a new fate for myself.

I chose to harness the power of the Infinite Universe and believe wholeheartedly that it was greater than any test result. I changed my thinking from, "I can't walk or speak," to "I can't walk or speak at this moment, but I *will*."

Some days later, I spoke.

I was moved to a ward in which my only view was a brick wall. It felt worse than a prison cell and I longed to see flowers and the sky. My voice had returned, but my body and spirit felt disconnected from the outside world.

Again, I realized lying in that hospital bed, that I couldn't see the sky, but I could picture it. It's interesting that when our lives are in critical danger, we need critical thinking the most. Yet, it's in those moments that critical thinking seems to disappear.

Through sheer determination to choose my own fate and with

the help of critical thinking, I gradually regained my ability to walk and communicate. Critical thinking allowed me to navigate the overwhelming fear and uncertainty, and regain control of my body, turning a seemingly impossible situation into a series of challenges I could face head-on.

You see, critical thinking is *a heartfelt decision*. No matter what's happening to you, you can choose to direct your own thoughts in an empowered and productive way. It is the seat of your free will and allows you to look beyond the surface and into the realm of possibilities. Even when the odds are stacked against you, the choice to think empowered thoughts is often the difference between despair and hope, between surrendering and fighting, between failure and success.

In that hospital I made a choice to ignore the fact that no one was communicating with me and to have a powerful, life-altering communication with myself!

THE POWER OF *CHOICE*

You're a human being, so I can assume that you've suffered. It's part of the human condition. I can assume that at one time or another, your body experienced pain or illness.

I can also assume that you've felt sad and betrayed and at some point had your heart broken.

It's in these moments that being a human becomes an extreme sport and we are tasked with going to battle not with illness or the people who have hurt us, but with ourselves.

It is only ever about us, and our willingness to *decide* to heal, to grow, to process information, to look for patterns, to draw from the source of our inner strength, and to at last, with blood in our hair and bruises on our hearts, declare with a scratchy, battered voice, "*No more. I choose to heal.*"

I remember a day when my pain was at an all-time high. I was sitting in the dark, crying, when I caught my reflection in the window. My appearance startled me. My face was red and swollen.

Despair had drawn new lines on my face and that, with my disheveled hair, made me look much older than I was.

I barely recognized the woman staring back at me and I had to again remember that when it seems that we have nothing left, if we have our minds, there is always hope.

I whispered to myself, "How can I get out of this state?"

It was a turning point and from that moment, "how can I" became three of the most powerful words I could speak.

How often, during turmoil, have you found yourself saying, "How can this be! How can I get through!" What you might now notice is that in our despair, we tend to say these things as statements, not questions, leaving no room for answers to be whispered to us.

As a statement, there is no room for hope.

Once I realized that and began to place a question mark at the end of my "how can I" sentences, everything changed.

When we ask a question, our brains immediately go to work, sifting through memories, knowledge, and experiences to find an answer. It is a kind of internal search engine, trying to connect the dots and provide us with what's most useful and guide us toward solutions.

When I finally stopped lamenting, "How can I get through this!" and changed it to, "How can I get through this?" the answers came quickly.

"Sit up."

"Stop crying."

"Take a shower and change your clothes."

I jumped off the stool and did as my mind directed. Asking, "How can I?" provided me with clear and manageable baby steps to healing.

It was a push to *anything* other than wallowing. Since that moment, I have had numerous strategic conversations with my clients and become a Life Mastery Coach/Consultant.

But none of that would have been possible, had I not learned the power of choice.

I could choose to employ the magic of critical thinking. I could choose to ask for and follow the next step, and the one after that. I could choose, even in moments of total uncertainty, to have powerful and strategic conversations with myself.

THE POWER OF *DISCIPLINE*

Deciding your own fate is not something you do once. It's a choice you'll need to make again and again, and it will show up in the most mundane ways and in the most serious.

You decide your own fate when you accept or reject an invitation; when you decide to drive this way or that; when you choose to believe a doctor's diagnosis or take healing into your own hands.

Yet, deploying the power of choice isn't always enough. Often our fate rests on our level of *discipline.*

A while back, I awoke one day with crippling arthritis so painful, I struggled to walk. I visited the doctor who sent me for x-rays and said, "We're going to have to take out your knees and replace them. But your new knees will have a shelf-life, so you'll need to have them replaced again in a few years and the recovery is lengthy and difficult."

I was in shock. This was not what I wanted. My mind immediately returned to the moment I laid on the trolley in the dark hallway of the hospital and it hit me. I had been there, done that, bought the t-shirt!

I could accept his dismal treatment plan.

Or I could *decide* on a different one.

I told him 'No thank you' and hobbled out of his consulting room, aware that I was now in a pickle with no treatment plan, but fully confident that with the help of critical thinking, I would find one. And that's when the three powerful words came to mind.

How can I?

How can I cure this pain?

Research.

I found doctors who had cured arthritis without knee

replacement surgery. I poured over their research and applied every exercise they had used in their studies.

Each week, I added a new task to strengthen myself. I couldn't step up onto the curb, so I began by putting a piece of paper on the floor as my first increment and stepped over it. Next, I added a book and stepped onto it. Little by little I added more books until the pile of books was the height of the curb and I repeated this until the day I could walk outside and step onto the actual curb without wincing in pain!

I was blown away by how the combination of choice and discipline had rewired my body. I had been impersonating a vegetable and then walked and talked again. I had healed my knees without surgery. Eventually, I would bounce back from brain surgery using these same tactics.

I even applied choice and discipline to completely change my diet and wrote a book called *My Brilliant Body*.

You might see your mind like a genie in a bottle. It can grant wishes or take them away. It can seem like a benevolent genie or a cruel one. How your mind behaves, however, is entirely up to you. This is perhaps the most empowering realization of all. Your mind awaits your direction.

You, my friend, are the genie.

THE POWER OF *TENDING* YOUR GARDEN

"It's not working.

"I have tried to think positively, but bad things still happen and I'm still unhappy."

I can't tell you how often I have heard things like this from my clients and it's then that I must remind them that growth is not a linear process. When you think of a growth trajectory, you might picture a chart in which an arrow goes in an upward direction.

True growth, however, is more like a roller coaster! Consider a garden. It would be easy if all we had to do was plant a bunch of seeds and watch them grow in an upward direction but it's much more complicated than that.

A garden is not a one-time or linear process but rather a cycle of planting, weeding, pruning, and repotting, each step vital to its growth and beauty. Just as a garden requires ongoing care and strategy, so does life. There are moments in which you will plant new seeds of hope, and times you will need to weed out negativity, prune away what no longer serves you and repot yourself into new environments where you can thrive.

Choosing to think positively and practice discipline is not a one-time action leading to some kind of promised land. It is a chosen way of life. It is a continuous journey of nurturing yourself, adapting to change and renewing your thoughts over and over again. Without the ongoing process of planting, watering, tending and weeding we are left with a barren field of dirt that yields little nourishment or reward.

Your life is your garden. Tend it well.

THE POWER OF *YOU*

One thing we can all agree on is that being a human being is a rather challenging adventure.

It's beautiful and painful and alternately crushing and bountiful. None of us can escape the contrast that comes with being alive, but we can escape the suffering.

We can choose to use our minds and think our way to a more empowered state of being. We don't have to hit rock bottom or suffer indignities. You can use your power of choice and the magic of discipline to completely rewrite your story.

As you read this, I am tending to two gardens, the one that is my life, and the one in my yard. I remember how disconnected and sad I felt in the hospital room staring at a brick wall. My plan is to livestream the planting and tending of my garden so that people who are incapacitated have a view that inspires them; a view that reminds them that regeneration is indeed possible!

I live in Scotland and our landscape is unique in that it is framed by a contrasting combination of rugged highlands and deep, glacially carved lochs. There is a clear juxtaposition of high mountainous terrain and tranquil, deep lakes all of it steeped in ancient folklore and colorful stories.

That's life, isn't it? Highs and lows, peaks and valleys and rich stories of love, loss and transformation.

As I reflect on my journey, I know now that our power to think, choose, and act is the key to reclaiming our lives again and again. In the darkest corridors, in the solitude of hospital rooms, and in the face of overwhelming odds, I found that the cure for pain, both emotional and physical, isn't found in a medicine bottle but in the potent power of our minds.

We simply need to remember that our minds bend to our will and can become our greatest enemy or our greatest ally.

Remember, we are gardens. We bend to the light. We thrive with attention. We can grow and regenerate as the seasons change. There may be periods of drought and decay, but with intention, we will break through, flourish and grow.

If you harness the boundless power of your thoughts, you'll find you can transform every trial into a story of strength and renewal.

About J ' X

As a certified Life Mastery Consultant with the Life Mastery Institute, the premier training centre for transformational coaching. J ' X can help you create a life that you absolutely love living.

For over forty-five years J ' X has studied and implemented transformational success principles. Acquiring, despite much mental and physical trauma, a wealth of valuable experience through creating works of art music literature and design. As well as mentoring others to tap into their potential and flourish despite their circumstances. As Architectural Designer in residence at Robert Gordon University she mentored students both for studio support and for live architectural projects. Based on art project community gardens that she devised and ran.

J ' X worked in the prestigious Scottish Design Centre in Glasgow, before going freelance.

As an artist she was published by Cannes Down Press and exhibited throughout the UK, including Mandel's in London. She won the social housing Helen McGregor Award. And has been a voluntary chair or vice chair of a major housing association continuously for over fifteen years. During which time she was involved in the designing and delivering of an urban village. She has written 4 books and a play; all focused on supporting and developing the human potential. She shared a stage with Cliff Hague, prior Royal Town Planning Institute president, talking about the importance of planning on people's mental and physical health.

Ever mindful of the environment J ' X established the first SEPA registered domestic lightbulb recycling and battery collection centre in the UK. Visiting schools to talk about sustainability before sustainability was a thing.

Now J ' X is focused on helping people unfold their inner potential in order to live their dream life. To this end she has developed what she calls art-yoga. Currently she is in the early stages of establishing her Garden of Life project. Where the garden acts as a living canvas for art-yoga. A place for reconnecting people to nature and each other. A place for sharing and supporting an ongoing legacy of designing and living a life you absolutely love.

J ' X believes that it is never too soon or too late to realise that every circumstance and situation, every strategic conversation is an opportunity to blossom into the life of your dreams.

To learn more about working with J ' X, go to isobydesign.org.

CHAPTER 11

THE LANGUAGE OF LEADERSHIP

The Five Feelings That Drive Successful Conversations

By Gina Caruso-Hussar

"I'm done," I whispered to no one at all. "I'm done. I'm done. I'm done."

I woke up feeling heavy and sluggish, dreading the day ahead. I'm a single mom of three and have owned a copywriting and branding company for the last twelve years. For five of those years, I had worked with an eight-figure client who was slowly draining the life out of me.

The dilemma was that this client, while notoriously difficult to work with, paid *extremely* well.

That morning, I could no longer ignore what needed to be done. I walked away from a very high monthly retainer because my intuition told me to. The same intuition that landed this lucrative contract when I needed it was now telling me to let it go.

That's the funny thing about intuition. It doesn't support logic, it almost always requires you to get uncomfortable, and yet it's never wrong.

I've been empathic and intuitive my whole life. I've never come out and said it because too many people think of an intuitive as a dime store psychic with a crystal ball and a fake accent.

But here are a just a few things my empathy and intuition have led me to do:

- I wrote an eBook for a client that generated more than $370,000.

- I've ghostwritten more than fifty books, including best sellers.

- I've written sales funnels that have generated multiple six figures.

- I wrote an event campaign that contributed to $962,000 in sales in one weekend.

- I created a magazine and worked with celebrities such as the cast of *Dancing with the Stars*, Pamela Anderson, and MTV.

- I gave speeches and sold more than $50,000 worth of product from the stage in just twenty minutes. The words didn't come from my brain but from my ability to read what the audience needed.

I've had people say to me, "Wow. You're brilliant!"

I'm not. I've just learned to leverage my soft skills instead of seeing them as a hindrance. I've learned, after years of being called "too sensitive" that I can succeed not despite my sensitivity but *because* of it.

Soft skills in sales and negotiation are critical because they shape the dynamics that can make or break a deal. In fact, research shows that 85% of success comes from soft skills, while only 15 percent is attributed to technical knowledge.

Soft skills are not the *opposite* of intellect. They are a *form* of intellect, and I would argue, the most vital form.

The use of soft skills in strategic conversations is simply the act of grabbing knowledge from a realm that is universally understood—human behavior.

I credit my soft skills for helping me build a six-figure company from scratch. Even if you've never heard of me, there's a chance I've sold you something. For the last several years I've worked as a brand strategist and copywriter for some of the most well-known names in the coaching and business development industries.

What I've found is that one thing that most successful people have in common is that they know how to lead a conversation with empathy, and more importantly, they understand that there is *always* a conversation in play...

Conversations Happen Everywhere

A while back I stumbled onto a website for an energy healer. The site's colors were black and deep red. She was using words like "execute the healing," which felt a bit... off. Words, after all, hold a frequency. Because the aesthetics didn't match the title she'd given herself, I felt I had to keep scrolling to figure it out.

Then of course I remembered I didn't have time for that and I x'd out. She may have been a miracle worker, but her branding created confusion. You see the second a person stumbles on your website, a conversation has begun.

Sure, it's happening primarily in the head of the viewer, but there is indeed a back-and-forth exchange. You've presented a point of view, and they're considering it, judging it, and feeling it out in search of alignment. The same is true if you write a book or host a podcast. You are in a conversation with an audience. The message, the energy, and the aesthetics must work together in harmony. If they don't, you're leaving money on the table. The dark colors on the healer's site coupled with the disconnected language didn't convince me that this woman could heal anyone. Instead, I pictured her kicking someone's ass.

Every interaction in which a message is communicated to an audience, whether face-to-face, virtual, or over the airwaves, is a form of conversation—and first impression journeys are vital.

The key to initiating powerful conversations is to create a journey for the audience that elicits good feelings. Whether that audience is comprised of thousands of people or just one, you want to think about the impression you'd like to leave. What does someone *feel* after experiencing you?

If you want to learn how to master the art of the audience journey, look at Disney.

Disney knows that if they can get you to *feel* something, you'll buy. They know if they do their job right, your *emotions* will make you forget about your *transactions*. They spend millions of dollars on technology, but their commercials are about families, love, and once in a lifetime memories. They've done that so well that you find yourself justifying the purchase of a thirty-dollar lollipop that looks like Cinderella's head because they've activated your core emotions. Those feel-good hormones are Disney's swag bag.

It's not manipulative, it's strategic. It demonstrates a solid understanding of how humans operate, decide, and *feel*.

As you enter any conversation, be intentional. How do you welcome your audience? What do you offer them to make them feel cared for?

And can you answer the Gateway questions?

THE GATEWAY QUESTIONS

Before I enter any conversation, whether it's a face-to-face meeting or a sales page I'm writing, I ask myself two questions.

The first is: "What problem do you solve that a Google search can't?"

With so much free content on the web, it's extra hard to inspire people to listen to you. Why listen to anyone when Google and YouTube can tell you everything about anything in three seconds and for free?

That's why it's imperative to know the differentiating *human* element you bring to the table.

I had a financial adviser client who found a little-known benefit for veterans. Anyone could've googled the benefit and found tons of information, but it was *very* complicated. My client offered to apply for the benefit on her clients' behalf. Which leads to the second question:

What are you *really* offering?

In the case of the client I just mentioned, she was offering less stress and peace of mind. When you know the emotional payoff your audience wants, you can steer the conversation in the direction it needs to go.

The best way to do that is to tune in to the soft skills that all of us have access to and allow them to do the heavy lifting *for* you.

Ever heard of the book *The 5 Love Languages*? The idea is that by understanding your partner's love language, you can build a stronger relationship.

What I've spent my career honing are *The 5 Leadership Languages*.

Whether you're speaking to someone across a table or across the current of the internet, the 5 Leadership Languages are the five feelings the other party must feel in order to respond to you.

By understanding a little behavioral psychology, you'll be strongly positioned to build connections.

And *connection* is the bridge to results.

THE 5 LEADERSHIP LANGUAGES

1. Connection

Connection says, "I understand where you're coming from."

Connection is key to building trust and rapport. When the person you're speaking to believes that you understand their needs and challenges, they're more likely to trust your suggestions.

You can build connection by restating their frustration: "What I'm getting is that you're determined to stop losing money on this outdated business model, is that accurate?"

Or, if the conversation is happening through marketing copy it might say: "Worried that it's too late to find your soulmate and that there are no good men left?"

And then, restating their desire: "I'm guessing it would feel better to never again wonder where your next dollar is coming from because your sales calls always convert."

The language of connection says, "I've listened, and I understand exactly what your goal is here."

2. Empathy

Empathy says, "Not only do I know what you're going through, but I understand how what you're going through makes you feel."

Empathetic language ties *their* problem to *your* solution. Now, I'm going to provide an example used in marketing copy, but the principle applies to any conversation in any room, through any medium. Empathy and permission are *key*.

Example:

"I get it. It's gut wrenching to wonder if you'll ever make money doing what you love or if you'll have to give up."

"So often, just one small shift needs to be made. That's exactly what happened to me. I was struggling, spending ten to twelve hours a day chasing down clients and for little in return. I was so ashamed every time a friend asked me how it was going. Then I made one simple shift that doubled my income in thirty days. Would you like to know what the shift was?"

Start with empathy as you make your way to building curiosity.

Only once you've asked permission to share can you begin to speak the third language.

3. Trust

Trust says, "I have a solution for you. I know it will help."

Your solution is your chance to establish resonance and demonstrate your expertise. This is empathy in action and a chance for you to be in service.

At this point in the conversation, you want to put your own agenda aside and be as generous as possible. A conversation is a sacred relationship and must be honored as such. We're asking to take up time, space and attention in their world.

As you share your solution, you want to present it not as a bartering tool or alternative, but as a *gift*.

You want them to say two things, "Wow. I cannot believe they offered that!" *and* "How can we make that happen?"

The Language of Trust offers a solution that tends to their problem thoroughly and generously while leaving them with just enough tension to *ask* for your leadership.

Then, we want them to feel good about that decision which is why the next language is vitally important...

4. Inspiration

When we speak the language of inspiration, we're saying, "Here's what's possible for *you*."

A common mistake people make in a strategic conversation is that they pour time into the strategy, the game plan and the technical execution and maybe even use their soft skills to build trust and then—they stop.

Ever been stood up on a date?

That's how your audience feels if you fail to inspire.

This happens when the leader fails to lead all the way through. You've done all the right things. You've got them where you want them. So, you shift out of soft skills and into "all business." You've left their side and gone back to your own and in doing so, trust is fractured and doubt creeps in. You must intuit what they need to hear to feel good about their decision to work with you.

The key is to stay in service and one of the best ways to do this is through story.

Compare these emails from two health consultants:

"I'm the leading health coach in this industry. I've helped hundreds of people lose weight. We'll meet twice a month, and you'll get my free meal plan. The cost is $2000 but it's worth every penny."

Versus:

"It came. The dreaded invitation to your high school reunion. And all you can think is 'I cannot go looking like this.'

"I remember that feeling. My son's parents' night for football was coming up and I knew that at half time, I'd have to walk out onto the field for a picture. I couldn't imagine what people might be thinking (or worse, saying) as I made my way to him, a good 50 pounds overweight. The thought I couldn't get out of my head was this—would my son be as embarrassed as I was? I couldn't go there like that.

"And you don't have to either. Would you like me to show you exactly how you can lose 10 pounds in less than 30 days?"

Which one felt more emotional and inspiring? Which one didn't mention the coach at all but rather built a bridge to the emotions and desires of the receiver?

Too many people make the mistake of thinking that story has no place in business. But if business is being conducted by humans, and until the robots fully take over it still is, then human conventions work.

When you leverage stories, you don't just close deals—you open doors.

5. Commitment

Commitment says, "I'll do everything I can to help."

There's a misconception that your number one goal should be to get a commitment from your prospect. However, the commitment that seals the deal doesn't come from the other party, but from *you*. Stay in the seat of the leader no matter what's happening, or how challenging it gets. My old neighbor used to say, "Judas ate too." If you're familiar with the Last Supper, Judas betrayed Jesus but Jesus still invited him to dinner. Judas's behavior did not dilute Jesus's kind character.

You don't have to be religious to get it. If you consider yourself a leader, *lead*; not just when things are going smoothly; not just when people are doing what you want them to do. Lead not because it's your job but because it's your character; not because it's what you *do*, but because it's who you *are*.

Soft Is a Superpower

"One who scorns the power of intuition will never rise above the ranks of journeyman calculator.... We are slowed down sound and light waves.... We are souls dressed up in sacred biochemical garments and our bodies are the instruments through which our souls play their music."

Those words weren't written by a spiritual hippie working a booth at a psychic festival. They were written by Albert Einstein.

Even Einstein knew that often the path to success cannot be found in data and mechanics.

When facts and evidence fail, the answers you seek may lie beyond the edges of intellectual reasoning. We are born with the power to empathize and attune to the energy fields of those around us.

Your rational mind is limited by what you intellectually know. Your intuitive mind is not limited by *anything*.

When we dare to trust the unseen forces of empathy, intuition, and connection, we unlock the potential to transform not just conversations, but lives.

About Gina

Gina Caruso-Hussar began her career as a marketing executive for Saks Fifth Avenue and is now a best-selling author, award-winning writer, and founder of Higher Media Group, a creative direction and personal development company that fuses the powerful science of energetics with the creative process to help clients discover their highest potential in life and business. Gina has worked with some of the top coaches in the personal development and business coaching industries to ensure that purpose, brand messaging, content strategy and energy blend together for a solid ascension plan that aligns with each client's values, vision and personal ecology.

In 2025, Omari Energetics will at last be open to the public. Clients will be able to visit the studio for branding, copywriting and business energetics or the sanctuary for energy healing, intuitive guidance and bibliotherapy.

Gina has had the pleasure of working with celebrities such as the cast of *Dancing With the Stars*, Pamela Anderson, Lauren Conrad, the rock group Karmin, Dita Von Teese, Camila Alves, Jack Canfield and Kathy Ireland and has been featured in The Huffington Post, *Gladys Magazine*, and *Beverly Hills Magazine*.

As a certified Law of Attraction Coach, certified Business Consultant, certified energy healer, and metaphysician, she has spent the last several years working with a who's who list of self-help authors, personal development coaches, entrepreneurs and speakers, helping them to reach ultimate states of alignment, clarity and abundance by way of conscious business consulting and energetic calibration.

With an eye toward integration, she and her team developed multiple assessments that lead clients through a journey to self-awareness as a bridge to growth.

Her clients are privy to a unique cross-disciplinary approach and custom-curated "prescriptions" that might include everything from custom re-brands and content strategy to intuitive guidance, Spiritual Coaching and Energy Work.

To connect with Gina, visit www.ginahussar.com or send an email to gchussar@live.com.

CHAPTER 12

THE S-WORD

By Drew Rowley

You know him. He appears suddenly, as if he could smell you when you parked. Pleated pants. Tucked-in polo. Every hair slicked into place and that uncomfortably large, toothy smile striding straight toward you.

The salesman.

Have you ever been in sales? Ever sat through an eight-hour grind, making call after call, getting hung up on, cursed at, even threatened for having the audacity to sell health insurance? Or maybe you have fallen for a trap. Some fast-talking, pushy sales-person high-pressured you into buying something that, even while you were signing on the line, made your stomach feel sick? It's a brutal reality for all of us: You cannot avoid salespeople.

I have bad news for you. At some point we are *all* salespeople, whether we're trying to impress a date or convincing the kids to eat their veggies. When you want something from another person, how do you get it?

Sales.

Most people react as if *salesperson* is a four-letter word. I, myself, am that dreaded salesman. Like the devil himself, I relentlessly stalk my prey and lure them into my iron clad traps. At least, that's what my mind sells me about what others think of me before we have a chance to talk. For *years* my own stomach felt sick when-ever someone asked me what I do for a living. "Marketing" I would say, or perhaps, the more effervescent, "Strategic Partnership

Negotiation." I would say pretty much anything to avoid saying I was in "sales."

Yet the reality is, you can't make it through life without being a salesperson. Every day we encounter situations that require us to negotiate.

Every day, we are advocating for our needs and desires, and we start honing this skill as soon as we can talk and some would argue, even before that.

Exhibit A: the toddler.

Toddlers are genius negotiators.

When my youngest child was small, he wanted a cookie. With dinner in the oven, I said "no," which launched a debate of epic proportion in which he showed the tenacity of a seasoned business shark.

When I said the first no, he simply asked in different words. When I said no again, he asked in a different tone of voice. When I said no a third time, he started telling me why I was wrong and why the cookie mattered so much. Ever seen Matteo, the "Listen Linda" kid on YouTube? (If not, you've missed a treat; go check it out!) Well, this was like that—my kid was using vocabulary and negotiation tactics beyond his years.

My noes only motivated him to get more creative in his request.

What can we learn from toddlers?

1. Conviction.

2. Unwavering commitment to the end-goal.

3. Belief that anything is possible if you get creative in your plan and never take your eyes off the prize.

From a young age, we instinctively understand that influencing others helps us navigate the world. It's a basic survival and social skill that evolves as we grow, shaping our interactions and relationships.

Now, what toddlers *lack* are three critical principles of conscious persuasion: preparation, connection and mindfulness.

So, before you vow to never sell anything to avoid coming across as a fast talker in a cheap suit, keep reading. I'll tell you how to have strategic, conscious conversations that embody the principle I have built my career on, which is this: Selling = Service.

If I'm afraid to sell or negotiate, the needle never moves. The situation is never served. *Nobody* gets a cookie.

PREPARATION

It has been said that interest is the sincerest form of respect.

If I really want to be of service to someone, I've got to get to know them, understand their motivations and hopefully, craft a conversation that meets their needs. Before I get on the phone with a potential client, I spend a *minimum* of fifteen minutes cyber-stalking them for points of connection. If I notice on LinkedIn that they went to Michigan State I can assume that a mention of the Spartan's latest conquest might build quick rapport. People like to talk about themselves and when you are prepared with a personal fact, it humanizes the conversation. Suddenly, I'm no longer viewed as adversarial, but a potential business associate and, dare I say, friend? As Jeffrey Gitomer, author of *The Sales Bible*, says, "More sales are made with friendship than salesmanship."

Years ago I worked at 20th Century Fox and NBC Universal, responsible for strategic partnerships within consumer products, aka merchandise, aka tchotchkes. That Bart Simpson mug you drink your coffee in might be born out of a meeting I led. The Dunder Mifflin paper you're writing on? My team and I worked our butts off to make that happen! It wasn't easy. As you can imagine the creators of beloved shows such as *The Simpsons* or *The Office* were extremely protective of their brands, and it was our job to sell them our product ideas while reassuring them that we wouldn't cheapen their show. It was an exciting job that gave me the chance to work with some of the most creative minds in Hollywood including a few household names.

One of those was Jimmy Fallon.

It was 2010, and my meeting with Jimmy was scheduled for the morning after he hosted the Golden Globe Awards. I watched the awards, during which he did a number of remarkable impressions. Determined to be prepared, I made notes of my favorites so I could mention them during our call.

When Jimmy picked up the phone the next morning, I expected to have to persuade him that our work was worth his time, but it didn't go that way. Instead, Jimmy came to the call with a large list of ideas. He spoke for twenty minutes straight, sharing some favorite bits from his show, *Late Night with Jimmy Fallon*, and the ideas he had for morphing those bits into real-world products. He was the most prepared person, let alone celebrity, I've ever spoken to. I was already a fan, but Jimmy's preparation for our meeting demonstrated his understanding of *our* process and showed that he respected my time as much as I respected his. Our mutual commitment to being prepared led to several successful and never-done-before products landing on store shelves, including a New York Times bestseller.

Preparation is also important when things *don't* go as smoothly.

Recently, I had a client paying for services in installments. Halfway through, after we had already delivered 90 percent of the work, the client wanted to back out of the remaining payments which would mean lost profits of nearly $10,000! I wasn't about to let that happen. Before our meeting, I did my best to reflect on what their experience of our company had been. Noodling all potential reasons they might want to sever ties and then crafting responses to each. I went through every component of our relationship to see where they might be perceiving lack of value. I reminded myself not to be angry at them, not to feel like they were trying to sleaze their way out of paying $10,000. The key is to treat the *situation* as the enemy, not the client. It's never you against them, it's you and them against a situation gone rogue.

I was kind, I was prepared, and I didn't lose!

CONNECTION

Marshall B. Rosenberg was a world-renowned peacemaker who developed the art of non-violent communication. His work was not solely centered around making sure we didn't all punch each other during an argument, but rather that we took care to understand the emotions and principles of the other party so we could work towards common ground. One of the best ways to do that and to ensure that we are conversing with emotional integrity is to practice empathy.

Rosenberg once said that "Empathy is a respectful understanding of what others are experiencing." Every encounter we have is a chance to display empathy or withhold it. The very best leaders understand that empathy is vital to impact.

Years ago, while attending the University of Southern California, I was doing a work study with the events office and we had an incredible speaker at one of our events: former President, George Bush senior. Politics aside, it was exciting. I was just a young kid from Parker, Colorado who suddenly found himself briefing Secret Service agents so they could ensure the President's safety. As he was walking into the event, I had the chance to meet President Bush. He looked me right in the eyes and said, "Hello Drew! Thank you so much for being here!" He spoke to me as though we had known each other our entire lives. It was only a twenty-second conversation, and I was captivated. He must have understood I was nervous and calmed my nerves by glancing at my name tag (although I never actually *saw* him do it) and using my first name. His greeting put me instantly at ease. It didn't feel like meeting him for the first time, but rather seeing him again after a long separation. It was brilliant. I felt *seen*. To this day whether I'm talking to a cashier, a server or a million-dollar client, I try to invoke this tactic to help them feel seen.

I had the chance years later to deploy this kind of tactical empathy when I was working with a universally feared executive of *The Simpsons*. Gracie Films was the name of the production company that owned the show, and we couldn't sneeze without their approval. Any product idea we had was put through a series of checks and balances that seemed to take forever, unpredictably and consistently delaying the process. They rejected seven-figure deals from Monster.com (which was still big at the time) and Apple. Apple for crying out loud! It took *months* to get some deals approved, and it was a constant challenge. I knew that if I wanted to expedite my deals, I would need to turn the gatekeeper into an ally. I would need to befriend the executive whom everyone else avoided, not to get her on my side, but to understand her challenges.

Why did she make it so hard?

What was her experience of my team and the process?

Why did everything really take so long and seem to require the blood of a first born to get anything pushed through?

After one of my first calls with her, I learned that she was held personally responsible for protecting this multimillion-dollar beloved brand and was the "middleman" for *every* request that came through the office. The volume of things she had to deal with sounded exhausting. I empathized with the sheer overwhelm she must feel daily and felt genuine compassion for the human behind the scary reputation. That one phone call led to a wonderful working relationship, and it no longer took months to get my deals approved.

Somehow my requests always landed at the top of her pile.

MINDFULNESS

Many years ago, while navigating a huge personal challenge, I started to practice mindfulness. I had been introduced to the work of Eckhart Tolle and his book *A New Earth*, which is essentially a love letter to the art of living in the present moment.

Meditation did not come easily to me. I started with thirty seconds of silence, but ten seconds in, the intrusive thoughts would begin.

"Did I send that email? Was that server insulting me? Is that bacon I smell?"

Eventually, I trained myself to accept those thoughts, thinking to myself, "It's ok to think that, but it's not what I'm doing *right now*. I can always come back to that, if it's still important later," and I would return to my breath, instantly snapping me back into the present moment. Why does mindfulness matter?

Because we are mostly a bunch of impatient toddlers who can't wait to hear ourselves talk! Whether you are selling a product, negotiating a contract or talking to your spouse, the temptation to 'wait to talk' is huge. Most of the time we are not present enough to truly listen to what the other person is saying. Instead, as they talk, we are forming our response in our minds and impatiently waiting for our turn to speak up. If you aren't present, you aren't listening and if you aren't listening you are losing.

It might not be intentional, but it's true, nonetheless. When someone is speaking to you, they are giving you the most valuable thing they have to offer... their *time*.

If you can train yourself to honor that gift with gratitude by being fully present while actively listening to them, they will feel it and return the respect.

Essentially, make sure your thoughts are in the same place as your feet. If you're too busy spinning a response to hear what they're saying, you will miss important details; and details are clues to common ground.

BEING HUMAN IS A GIVEN; HUMANITY IS A CHOICE

We tend to move through the world with labels preceding us.

He's a salesman; she's a producer; he's a father. She's tough; he's weird. She has a reputation. He is an egomaniac. She's rich; he's poor.

Yet underneath all these arbitrary labels we all have one thing in common: We are human beings.

Human beings have an innate need to be seen, heard, and

validated. We also have a built-in need for connection. Regardless of what side of the table you're on, you and the person across from you share a need for community. In fact, research suggests that connection is essential to our survival. If you can remember that you realize that the goal is never to win, but to *connect* over a shared purpose.

Whether you're working a million-dollar deal or trying to get your kid to go to bed, that shift from "winning" to "connecting" sets the stage for solutions that are richer and more rewarding than you could ever have achieved by focusing solely on your own wants.

In the end the secret to successful conversations lies in the humanity you bring to the table. Every interaction can be an act of service when you prioritize the needs of the other person, seek to understand their perspective, and aim to create value.

I am proud to say that I have worked hard to make sure no one is rolling their eyes or inwardly groaning when they see my name pop up on caller ID. If they know me, they know I'm not calling to manipulate or cajole them.

If I've done my job right, they answer the phone cheerfully, knowing I'm going to listen to them with genuine curiosity, empathize with their challenges, and always, without fail, strive to *serve*.

About Drew

Drew Rowley is a seasoned sales and marketing executive with over twenty years of expertise in strategic partnership negotiation and business growth.

As vice president of Channel Sales at Big Red Media, Drew drove millions in revenue by expertly managing hundreds of vendor relationships, consistently surpassing sales targets by 125 percent. His dedication to helping others extends beyond the corporate world, having served as an addiction treatment advisor. In just three years, Drew guided nearly five hundred individuals through tailored programs, helping them embark on new paths to recovery.

Drew's career highlights include launching Lonely Planet's first-ever Consumer Products division. His negotiation prowess was demonstrated during his time at 20th Century Fox, where he expanded international licensing for beloved properties like *The Simpsons*, *Family Guy*, and *Ice Age*, growing business by 300 percent over five years. From there Drew served as Director of Global Consumer Products at NBC Universal. In this role, he achieved 40 percent year-over-year growth, overseeing iconic NBC and USA Network properties like *The Office* and *The Tonight Show with Jimmy Fallon*.

A proud graduate of the University of Southern California, where he earned his degree cum laude, Drew remains committed to uplifting others. He currently resides in Franklin, Tennessee, and enjoys retreating to the Colorado mountains whenever possible to connect with nature.

Connect with Drew:

linkedin.com/in/drewrowley

CHAPTER 13

HOPE OR MADNESS. HEAVEN OR HELL. WHAT WILL HUMANITY CHOOSE?

Be the Change

By Julie Meates

Voice of change; choose the good

GENERATIONS OF SLAVE TRADE

Etched into walls are blood, pain, and souls of millions persecuted, abused, and lost to slavery. Elmina Castle and Cape Coast Castle, often called "slave castles," sit on the coast of Ghana and at one time were vital ports for the transatlantic slave trade, transporting millions of enslaved humans to America, the Caribbean, and Brazil. Dark, filthy, airless dungeons are the site of vicious atrocities, illness, and torture, where beautiful African people were shipped from these whitewashed prisons through the door of "no return."

Elmina Castle, now a UNESCO site, depicts the horrors of history. Unfortunately, the slave trade is not a heinous injustice of the past safely tucked into history books. History repeats. The plague of modern slavery trade is stacked with disasters cascading like dominoes. The United Nations reports fifty million people are trapped in slavery worldwide, and it tears at your heart knowing the figures have risen by ten million from 2016–2021. Every country on earth is affected directly or through consumption and supply chains—including yours. Cobalt and slavery are a massive international dilemma.[1] We are all interconnected. No man is an island.

It's Happening All Around Us

Slavery is a word synonymous with the American Civil War, a terrible period of history most thought was eradicated. Few people realize; however, slavery has greater presence in American life *now* than ever. It's a fact no one wants to face, but until we do, it continues to permeate our lives, inching closer to home.

We've all heard countless stories that capture the physical and psychological imposition at the heart of slavery. These are stories of hideous, obscene violence: of mutilations, beatings, and rapes; of forcible separation of husbands and wives, parents, and children; of husbands forced to see their wives abused; and of wives forced to do unspeakable things. It is the story of power over liberty, of a people victimized and brutalized.

The more we work to raise awareness, the more we are blessed with synchronistic opportunities to do more. While filming a documentary *Hero* as coproducer with Nick Nanton and Remi Adeleke, a book on the bookshelf beside the computer jumped out, titled *Slavery, Resistance, Freedom*.[2]

The undeniable fact is history can repeat itself, for slavery still exists, in a modern-day disguise, around the world. Injustices perpetrated are like deadly missiles disguised as technological gadgets that fuel some of the deadliest wars, creating millions of refugees and millions of lost lives.

The Real Cost of Technology

In the movie *Let Them All Talk*, starring Meryl Streep, another character remarked, "We may be the last generation to see the stars." The night sky is now crowded with satellites, painting an apocalyptic scene—for high-speed internet and global broadband communication.

Ghana has become one of the world's hubs for electronic waste, "e-waste," with over sixty-two million tons generated globally in 2022 tainted with toxic substances, according to the UN—up 82 percent since 2010. E-waste includes smartphones, smartwatches, tablets, and computers thrown away. There is a tragic cost to e-waste's toxic footprint. As old devices are updated, they are shipped transatlantic, while this year alone Apple and Microsoft made in excess of trillions of dollars alone and US sits as one of the top ten electronic waste-producing countries in the world, along with China.

The worst part is millions of good people are complicit in this horror without even realizing it. This is especially true in the Democratic Republic of Congo, where more than seven million lives have been lost for greed and profit. Did you ever imagine something you use in your daily life might be contributing to the enslavement of a child?

The second Congo war, or Great War of Africa (1998–2003), was far and away the deadliest war of the twenty-first century and the greatest conflict since World War II. Still today the world's forgotten war people in eastern Congo face terror, political and economic instability, human rights abuses, and extreme exploitation. The human cost of coltan and cobalt contributes to modern-day slavery. Even in 2024, UN experts are alarmed at the widespread trafficking for sexual slavery and exploitation, even children. Armed groups continue to fight to profit from the sale of gold, cassiterite (tin), coltan (tantalum), and wolframite (tungsten). These "conflict minerals" are used in a wide range of products—including your computers, iPads, cell phones, Xboxes, and PlayStations.

Children in the Western world are being enslaved as well by the new technocracy, but it is an enslavement of the mind. Phone and video-game addiction are contributing to a massive decline in the physical and mental health crisis of our children, even affecting the brains of children, like *Glow Kids addicted to electronic cocaine*[3]— all of this is an intricately connected web of societal breakdown. As Kardaras (2022) so aptly states in his book, this is *Digital Madness*.[4]

Ironically parallel universes are interplaying like a pawn in the metaverse.

Tim Ballard's strength of the human spirit and the unwavering determination to bring justice to the voiceless puts a spotlight on human trafficking in documentaries such as *Sound of Freedom*.[5] Another documentary in conjunction with Operation Underground Railroad, called *It's Happening Right Here* [6], reveals a jarring inside look at the sex-trafficking trade that is infiltrating nearly every city and town in the United States.

It shows how technology has expanded the reach of predators through gaming and social media platforms, with topics such as online grooming, sextortion, and trafficking risks being explored.

In 2011, Free the Slaves released *The Congo Report: Slavery in Conflict Minerals*[7], exposing the grim realities of slavery in North Kivu province. The report documented forms of slavery linked to the ongoing conflict, including child soldiers and the abduction of civilians for forced labor and sexual slavery by illegal armed groups and rogue military units. The 2023 Global Slavery Index estimates that on any given day in 2021 around 407,000 people in the DRC were trapped in modern slavery—equating to a shocking rate of 4.5 people for every thousand citizens.

If people are willing to pay for these minerals to fuel our technology, companies will mine them, and more people will be captured and forced into slavery.

The United Nations reports over eight million people have been displaced—a staggering figure, making it the highest in Africa, one of the largest globally. Among these displaced are countless innocent children, their lives shattered by conflict. This crisis is driven by the ruthless destruction of homes and communities, with rape devastatingly used as a weapon of war.

Strategic Conversations and Courageous Leaders

How can you help from so far away? Sparking and supporting strategic conversations led by those willing to confront harsh truths is the answer. People such as Chris Voss, with his concept of "tactical empathy"[8]; Lema Shamamba; and Samantha Power, author of *The Problem from Hell*, are examples of leaders transforming conversations into action to combat modern slavery and genocide. As a wise man once said, "The only thing necessary for the triumph of evil is for good men to do nothing."

> Humanizing the people around you, and recognizing the needs, and interests of the people you are working with or representing.
>
> —BEN MEATES

According to UN News, round 160 million children worldwide—nearly one in ten—are forced into labor.[9] One in two hundred people is a slave.[10]

Courageous empathetic leaders can turn the impossible and disheartening to the possible and humanizing such as The Sentry[11], including John Prendergast, George Clooney, Ryan Gosling, and other upstanders.

LEMA'S STORY

Lema Shamamba escaped the Democratic Republic of the Congo when armed militias swept through her village, leaving a trail of devastation. After losing her husband to violence, Lema and her children fled, eventually spending years surviving under the shade of a mango tree. Now known as Mama Lema, she dedicates herself to easing the isolation felt by countless refugee families, bringing them a sense of community and support amid their unimaginable journeys.

Lema established the group Women of Hope. She was recognized for her work as a community leader in *Women Kind: New Zealand Women Making a Difference*, featuring change-making women across New Zealand, including ex-Prime Ministers Dame Jacinda Ardern and Helen Clark (now one of The Elders, a group of global leaders, including Richard Branson, set up by Nelson Mandela).

With a past scarred by conflict, coups, and rampant human rights abuses, the mining of coltan has driven millions of Lema's people from their homes. Armed men arrived with guns, brutalizing communities, raping women, taking children, and killing husbands in front of their wives. Lema's husband was among those lost to this violence, and afterward, she made the rare decision to attend university. There, she began protesting the slaughter of indigenous people, even daring to sign a memo to the governor. But when news spread the militia was targeting those who had signed, Lema took her youngest child and fled for safety.

Today, as a skilled embroiderer, Lema captures her people's suffering in her art, stitching the horrors of her homeland alongside the logos of the world's biggest tech companies. Her message is undeniable—revealing the brutal truths behind the technological comforts so many take for granted yet choose to ignore. But her work also carries a seed of hope, a call to action, challenging every viewer to step forward and do something, anything, to bring change.

A few international companies have signed an international covenant on ethical practice in their mining activities, but these covenants are often breached.

Countless armed groups with no regard for human life or dignity continue to enslave, brutalize, and kill those they cannot exploit, leaving entire communities in fear and grief. Lema implores us never to forget these ongoing atrocities in the north and east of the Democratic Republic of Congo, where the relentless mining of coltan and other precious minerals feeds the suffering.

Despite these horrors, Lema has dedicated herself to uplifting those devastated by conflict. She crafts and sells crocheted pieces to support the Amani Orphanage in Bweremana, DR Congo. Through her tireless work, she urges us all to confront the painful truth: The suffering in the DR Congo is woven into our daily lives, and we have the power—and the responsibility—to help change it.

What can the rest of us do? Plenty.

THOUGHTS AND PRAYERS ARE NOT ENOUGH!

So, what can good people do? An obvious solution is to stop mining the oceans and the Congo rainforest, the oxygen and carbon sink to the world, or to go back to where we were twenty years ago and stop the relentless proliferation of digital devices fueling wars and conflict and displacing millions of people from their land and food. Another solution is education. If we can spread the word of humanitarian crises, more good people may be catalysts for change.

In the eighteenth century, leaders such as the first Earl of Mansfield and William Wilberforce emerged as pioneers against the institution of slavery. Mansfield, England's most powerful judge, second to the king, delivered a landmark ruling in 1772 many saw as a declaration against the legality of slavery in England, marking a milestone in the abolitionist movement. Wilberforce, known as the "father" of British abolitionism, led a relentless parliamentary campaign, introducing twelve bills to ban the slave trade, finally succeeding on his last attempt. His famous quote is, "It is the true duty of every man to promote the happiness of his fellow creatures to the utmost of his power."

John Newton, once a slave trader himself, underwent a profound transformation that led him to become a passionate abolitionist. Newton's journey from trafficker of human lives to a repentant voice for justice illustrates the powerful possibility of change and redemption. His hymn, "Amazing Grace," often sung in protest and remembrance, reminds us of the darkness that even the most complicit can emerge from inspiring hope that, no matter one's past, each person has the capacity to stand against oppression. Newton's life and song echo through the ages, challenging us to confront our complicity in injustice and to seek a path of grace, courage, and moral clarity.

On January 1, 1863, amid the brutal throes of the Civil War, President Abraham Lincoln issued the Emancipation Proclamation—a historic decree that proclaimed, "All persons held as slaves" in the rebelling states "are, and henceforward shall be free." This bold move reframed the war as not only a fight to preserve the Union but also as a moral crusade against slavery. While the proclamation didn't immediately free all enslaved people, it marked a turning point, rallying abolitionists and strengthening the resolve of the Union. Lincoln's words resonated as a powerful step toward justice, inspiring a vision of freedom that would shape the nation's future.

And of course, the Ratification of the Thirteenth Amendment to the Constitution in December 1865 abolished slavery in the United States. Yet a century and a half later, the question of slavery again roils the water of American life. The last years of the twentieth century and the first years of the twenty-first century have witnessed an immense engagement with slavery.

Education is our most powerful weapon against the evils of this world.

We cannot allow the tireless work of historic leaders to unravel, nor can we stand by as history repeats itself. If we ignore these issues, we risk allowing injustices to grow in new forms. By supporting organizations that combat modern slavery and human trafficking, lobbying for stronger protections, being intentional about our technology consumption, and remaining vigilant in our communities, we can ensure progress made is not undone.

Everyone has a role to play, and with courage and empathy, we can push back. History may not be able to be rewritten, but the future can be guided in a new direction—one in which human life is honored, protected, and valued.

BE THE CHANGE

This chapter is a step in the direction of infinite possibilities.

It is vitally important to seek knowledge of historical and social circumstances related to culture as an essential, if sometimes challenging, first base for organizations and practitioners, countries and leaders working toward change.

Democratic Republic of the Congo President Félix Tshisekedi's recent legal battle against Apple over "blood minerals" sheds light on the cost of our technological advancements.[12] Minerals such as cobalt, essential to our smartphones and electric cars, are often mined under brutal conditions, where local workers, even children, face exploitation and violence. Tshisekedi's stand against Apple symbolizes a broader fight to protect Congolese resources and citizens from exploitation by global tech industries.

Make no mistake, one person can indeed make a difference. If everyone were to commit to making the journey from ignorance to awareness, to education, and finally, to action, lives would be saved, communities would be rebuilt, and this world would be a safer, more peaceful place.

As Nelson Mandela once said, "Sometimes it falls upon a generation *to be great*. You be that great generation. Let your greatness blossom. Of course, the task will not be easy. But not to do this would be a crime against humanity, against which I ask all humanity now to rise up."

Rise up. Don't look away. Millions of oppressed people are counting on us.

ENDNOTES

1. Victoria Audu, "The Back End of Genocide: How the Rush for Congo's Cobalt Is Killing Thousands," *The Republic*, November 19, 2023, https://republic.com.ng/october-november-2023/congo-cobalt-genocide/; "Modern Slavery: The True Cost of Cobalt Mining" Human Trafficking Search, 2017, https://humantraffickingsearch.org/resource/modern-slavery-the-true-cost-of-cobalt-mining/.

2. Gabor S. Boritt and Scott Hancock, eds., *Slavery, Resistance, Freedom* (Oxford University Press, 2009). See also John Prendergast et al., *Congo Stories: Battling Five Centuries of Exploitation and Greed* (Grand Central Publishing, 2018).

3. Nicholas Kardaras, *Glow Kids: How Screen Addiction Is Hijacking Our Kids—and How to Break the Trance* (St. Martin's Press, 2016).

4. Nicholas Kardaras, *Digital Madness: How Social Media Is Driving Our Mental Health Crisis—and How to Restore Our Sanity* (St. Martin's Press, 2022).

5. *Sound of Freedom*, directed by Alejandro Monteverde (Angel Studios, 2023).

6. *It's Happening Right Here*, directed by Nick Nanton (DNA Films, 2022).

7. *The Congo Report: Slavery in Conflict Minerals*, Free the Slaves, 2011, https://freetheslaves.net/wp-content/uploads/2015/03/The-Congo-Report-English.pdf.

8. *Tactical Empathy*, directed by Nick Nanton (DNA Films, 2024).

9. From Prendergast et al., *Congo Stories*, 21: "The rapid spread of cell phones, laptops, and video games sparked a spectacular increase in the price of the key raw materials in these gadgets—tin, tantalum, tungsten, and gold—and provided the fuel for what became known as Africa's First World War, in which over five million people perished"; "And today, as the electric car industry accelerates, the global demand for cobalt, the main ingredient in the lithium battery, has led to a spike in child labor in Congo's cobalt mines, which provide up to 60 percent of the world's supply." From Prendergast et al., *Congo Stories*, 45: "Few things in our modern era are as ubiquitous as the stable of electronics products that existed only in science fiction a few decades ago: cell phones, laptops, smart televisions, tablets, video games, etc. Global demand for these products began really generating steam in the 1990s, and that matters to Congo for two reasons. First, some of the raw materials needed to power these electronics products are sourced from Congo. Second, increases in global minerals prices have been connected to conflict in eastern Congo. For example, the biggest surge in demand for one mineral, tantalum, occurred just as Rwanda and Uganda were settling in for a long military occupation of much of the eastern third of Congo, which is where these minerals happen to be concentrated. Later in the 2000s, the steady increase in the price of tin and gold helped drive conflict in tin- and gold-producing areas. VIP Congo's 'conflict minerals' are primarily tin, tantalum, tungsten (the 3Ts), and gold. The 3Ts are indispensable to modern electronic devices. Tin functions as a solder on circuit boards in every electronic device we use. Tantalum stores electricity and is essential to portable electronics and high-speed processing devices. Every time you send a text message or open an app, tantalum is used. Tungsten enables cell phone vibration alerts." See also, "One in Every 10 Children Works—Instead of Going to School," UN News, June 12, 2023, https://news.un.org/en/story/2023/06/1137567.

10. Kate Hodal, "One in 200 People Is a Slave. Why?," *The Guardian*, February 25, 2019, https://www.theguardian.com/news/2019/feb/25/modern-slavery-trafficking-persons-one-in-200.

11. The Sentry (www.thesentry.org), was cofounded by George Clooney and John Prendergast.

12. "DRC Accuses Apple of Using Illegally Exploited Minerals From Conflict-Torn East," *Le Monde*, April 25, 2024, https://www.lemonde.fr/en/pixels/article/2024/04/25/drc-accuses-apple-of-using-illegally-exploited-minerals-from-conflict-torn-east_6669468_13.html.

About Julie

Julie Meates is a New Zealand-born humanitarian with a diverse career, endeavoring to bring more peace, kindness, and love into the world. Family is central to her life; she is married with three children and a large extended family.

Beginning her career as a teacher, Julie's passion for education and health led her to become a qualified social worker and counselor. Now a barrister and solicitor, she is actively pursuing post-graduate studies in education and health. Her commitment to community well-being is evident in her extensive volunteer work, driven by her paying kindness forward.

In 2002, Julie cofounded the Fulfil a Dream Foundation, with a vision, hope, and dream of strong and happy families; happy, healthy, vibrant communities; and wise and visionary leadership, uniting high-profile figures from all fields to empower individuals, families, and communities. She also was the chairperson of a Maori learning center (indigenous Kohanga Reo).

Julie is an eight-time best-selling author, coauthoring books such as *Pay It Forward*, with Brian Tracy; *Success*; *The Soul of Success, vol. 3*; *Turning Point*; *The Keys to Authenticity*; and *Mindset Matters* with Jack Canfield, along with *Never Give Up* with Dick Vitale and *Rise Up!* with Lisa Nichols. These books contribute to various causes, including non-profits dedicated to ending human trafficking and modern-day slavery, among others.

Julie joined Abundance Studios as a producer and worked on notable films, including *The Truth About Reading*; *Dickie V* documentary; *It's Happening Right Here*; *Tactical Empathy*; *Hero*; *Conquer 100*; *Brisa*; and Lisa Nichols' Broadway show, *When My Soul Speaks*. Now a two-time Telly Award recipient, Julie has also been a guest on TV shows such as *Hollywood Live*, *Times Square Today*, and *The Global Entrepreneurship Initiative's Summer Symposium* at Carnegie Hall. Her appearances have been featured on NBC, ABC, CBS, and FOX nationwide.

Julie has volunteered with Community Law's programme, in community justice panels that facilitate restorative justice to promptly address harm caused by offenders. She also served as the board secretary for the

United Nations executive in her Canterbury region and is involved with the Women of Hope Wake Up and Help Ourselves Trust Board.

Throughout her career Julie has volunteered with Women's Refuge, various NGOs, charitable organizations, and sport, musical, cultural, social, and community lead initiatives, empowering youth, families and communities. She held the position of vice president at Wairarapa International Communities Inc., engaged in community radio with local, national, and international broadcasts, and contributed to homelessness initiatives across the globe.

Julie Meates is a compassionate, kind, and inspiring leader, empowering diverse groups of people to achieve their goals.

CHAPTER 14

THE COURAGE TO BURN

Harnessing Your Inner Dialogue to Ignite Growth

By Monique Lam

W hen my phone buzzed, alerting me to a new notification, I almost ignored it. I was busy that day and assumed it was a social media update or a new email.

Yet something made me stop and read it.

"Did you request to change your email password?"

It was a simple question, but it stopped me dead in my tracks. I hadn't made that request. A creeping dread set in, but it wasn't the first time something like this had happened, so I figured I would log in, change my email password myself, and send the cybercriminal back to whatever dark corner of the internet he came from.

But I was too late.

That moment was the tip of the iceberg; it wasn't just my email they had infiltrated. My identity had already been stolen, and the scammers had launched a lateral attack, slipping through the cracks, obtaining my cell phone number and using it to invade all my other accounts. That notification was the first domino in a yearlong struggle to reclaim my life. It was 2018, and I had just taken a leap of faith and moved from Australia to Canada. I was excited to settle into a new chapter but instead had to abandon my pursuit of permanent residency and rush back to Australia to protect myself. My world turned upside down in an instant.

It was a brutal wake-up call, forcing me to confront the fragility of everything I'd taken for granted and reassess the direction of my life.

Every "ping!" from my cell phone brought with it a wave of panic. I changed my number, but the scammers came back. They accessed my bank account and stole my money but luckily, a second layer of protection had prevented them from making the final wire transfer.

By the time I got back to Australia, the world had been locked down by COVID-19. I was stuck in Australia for the next three years. During that time, I decided to go back to school and get another degree, this time in criminology and criminal justice. I was determined to know how the minds of criminals worked, and more importantly how to protect myself and my clients who were all in the tech industry.

When I finally made it back to Canada, I launched a marketing consulting company. The core of my work is understanding the challenges business owners face, counteract the frustrations and inefficiencies they've encountered with other agencies and map out a plan that gives them exactly what they need to protect their assets, grow their revenue and thrive in their market.

That year I spent reclaiming my own identity was a pivotal moment that forced me to reassess the value I wanted to bring into the world. Up until then, I'd been going through the motions, following the "normal" success trajectories and climbing all the right ladders.

But that notification became a line in the sand that caused me to really think about my life. It's sort of ironic. I had to lose myself to find myself.

I had to have my identity stolen to finally craft one that felt like *me*.

CHART YOUR OWN COURSE

Your journey in this world is influenced by the unique experiences you carry with you. We start from behind the lens of your individual understanding of the world, shaped by your history, friendships, educational background, and upbringing.

Then, something happens right under our noses without us even realizing.

The current of life sweeps us up and carries us along and even though there are times we briefly stop to question if we're going in the right direction, we dismiss those thoughts, because pushing against the current would be hard work.

Pretty soon, we've been carried to some distant shore we don't recognize, in relationships we don't want, taking jobs that are impressive but meaningless and wondering how we ended up there.

A truly well-lived life requires us to push against the current; to press pause and evaluate how we want to move through life, the value we want to bring to the world and the path that allows us to remain true to ourselves.

How do we do that?

How do we sift through noise and distraction and distill our life down to its essence?

We burn the haystack.

Burn the Haystack

You've heard the phrase "It's like finding a needle in a haystack," right?

Well, the best way to find that needle isn't to spend years arduously sifting through hay, it's to burn the haystack down. Under the ashes, the needle will be all that remains.

It's a radical method for getting rid of anything that distracts us from what ought to be our ultimate goal—creating the exact life we want to live.

We tend to focus our definition of success on vanity metrics and as someone who was raised in a family that valued high levels of achievement, I fell right into the trap, always striving to be number one and often hitting that mark both in school and in sales and management jobs that followed.

But vanity metrics, while nice on paper, give little meaning to our day-to-day levels of fulfillment.

Vanity metrics are the hay that's in the way. It's only in learning to have strategic conversations with yourself that you can finally burn it all down and get to the essence of who you are.

Here's how to do it.

Know your values.

Unless you've been living under a rock, you probably know that Taylor Swift is one of the most famous people in the world. Yet her success stems not from a big marketing budget but from something that doesn't cost her a dime—her authenticity. Taylor is committed to being as real as possible, to connecting to her fans and to standing as a symbol of fearless positivity even under the scrutiny of haters.

This fierce commitment to authenticity and an unwavering commitment to being vulnerable is the very thing that fills stadiums. She has outshined her peers, many of whom are tightly controlled by their public relations teams, because she refuses to let her image be molded by anyone else.

So, what can we learn from Taylor?

Know exactly who you are and remove anything that isn't that.

Once you know your core values, you can light your match and start burning away anything that doesn't align.

Maybe it's a job that looks good on paper but is sucking the life out of you, or a relationship that is comfortable but doesn't resonate with your future goals. Maybe it's time to abandon a goal that was made by a more impressionable version of yourself to make way for goals that are an exact fit to who you want to be.

Take time to figure out exactly what you stand for, and how a person with your set of values would choose to move through the world. What would they cultivate? What would they steer clear of?

And what would they need to burn all the way to the ground to become the person they want to be?

Once you know your values, know your *value.*

My first job in retail was selling computer products. I was the top salesperson and one of my coworkers was a teenage mother with two children and no formal education. One day, my boss pulled me into his office and told me he could only afford to keep one full-time employee. He asked if I thought he should keep me or my coworker.

Not only was I not going to take a full-time job away from a young mother, but I knew my value. I was one of the top 5 sales-people every week. He needed me more than I needed him, and I resented his choice to pit worker against worker.

I told him to give her the job.

Eventually word got around, and the office manager called and asked me to come back in a casual weekend position. I accepted that offer.

Because the weekend shift paid time and a *half,* and because I still knew how to be the top salesperson, I ended up making exactly what I made before but in two days instead of five! I am convinced that karma was rewarding me.

I stuck to my values and my *value,* and it paid off.

While you're burning hay, burn some bridges too.

One of the most mind-blowing facts I learned when I had my identity stolen is that often the perpetrator is someone you know.

In my case, it wasn't, but it did get me thinking… I looked at my phone and realized I had more than 300 contacts though I maybe speak to 20 people on a regular basis. Half of the people on that list, I couldn't even put a face to. One by one, I deleted con-tacts, deleted strangers from my social media accounts and got very discerning about who I spent time with.

If that sounds like it's not a big deal, try it. Your brain will immediately start bombarding you with "what-ifs."

"But I met that person on my last job—what if I need them again?"

"I know this person and I cut ties a long time ago, but what if they need help someday?"

If they are not a part of your present and unlikely to be a part of your future, don't be afraid to burn the bridge and make way for folks who should be!

You've probably heard of the book *The Life-Changing Magic of Tidying Up*, which encourages readers to get rid of anything that doesn't "spark joy."

Maybe it's people who no longer play a part or worse, play a toxic one. Maybe it's projects you've long lost your enthusiasm for. Take inventory of your life and the people and things in it.

If it doesn't spark joy or inspiration, burn it down.

You're getting closer and closer to the needle.

Dig Deep, and Then Deeper

Sometimes the needle you're looking for is buried deep under multiple layers of programming.

I recently had a client who couldn't seem to make any headway in his business. No matter what he tried, he couldn't scale. After just one conversation and a few deep questions, I could tell what was happening. He saw everyone around him as the enemy.

Potential partners were the enemy because they'd probably steal from him. Prospects were the enemy because they didn't understand the value of his offer. As he explained this, his shoulders slumped, and his face settled into a scowl.

It turns out that this client had quite a bit of childhood trauma and it prevented him from growing. Once we reframed his perspective on his childhood and opened his mind to receiving support and respect, everything changed. It turns out his biggest business problems had nothing to do with business at all.

Each of us is in an ecosystem.

We all contain moving parts that inform and affect one another so it's vital that we dig deep into why things are the way they are. The more willing we are to investigate what motivates us, what we fear, what we desire, the resentment we carry, and the outdated programming that's still running the show, the more hay we burn.

CHANGE YOUR APPROACH, NOT YOUR CHARACTER

One of the most common traits that happy, successful people share is their willingness to be adaptable. Sometimes we must change our approach to get ahead while holding onto the core of our character.

Failing to do so, and stubbornly adhering to our own way of doing things, is often a recipe for disaster.

An example of this is the story of Blockbuster Video. Once a giant in the video rental industry, Blockbuster failed to adapt to consumer preferences and technological advancements. While Netflix, Amazon, and other companies were quick to adapt to the demand for online streaming services, Blockbuster clung to its traditional brick-and-mortar business model which ultimately led to its downfall.

Blockbuster could have adhered to its promise of "the movies you want, for less" while also shifting into a digital model, but they didn't.

What about you?

Is there something you need to shift to move you closer to the life you want to live? Are you running your life from an old operating system that needs an update? Or perhaps you've hit a stalemate in a negotiation and it's time to try a different tactic?

Any belief, tool or system that you're holding onto past its expiration date becomes another layer of hay hiding your needle. We've got to be willing to take a hard look at what's not working and throw it out, no matter how attached we are to its familiarity.

When I had my identity stolen, I was in the midst of completely upheaving my life in Australia and moving to Canada. I returned to Australia because reclaiming my identity was my top priority. Then I realized that I wanted to change how I engaged with the world and left the hardware industry to study criminology and work in cybersecurity. Then through meeting tech business owners, I decided to open a marketing agency to help them grow. With every reinvention, I had to let something go.

This isn't about abandoning your principles. On the contrary, it's about evolution; a willingness to grow into the person you need to become to achieve your goal even if it means saying goodbye to the person you were.

LEAD WITH EMPATHY

When my mom escaped the war in her home country of Cambodia, she lost all but one of her siblings and both her parents. All of them were killed. She chose to marry young inside a refugee camp and eventually landed in Australia, though she spoke no English.

Despite those insurmountable odds, she is the kindest, most selfless person I know. She never lost her sense of empathy. From her I developed a knack for being the voice of reason and kindness in every situation, and I use that voice to have meaningful conversations with my clients. I listen respectfully, ask questions with genuine curiosity and use my own experience to help talk them off the ledge when it seems like everything is going south.

The hard reset I experienced in my own life helped me get clear about the value I could offer to others. Every experience, every reinvention took me deeper into knowing myself, which allowed me to form the basis of the proven system I use with my clients to help them narrow down their needs and desires and weed out any distraction that's hindering their goals.

That notification I got back in 2018 didn't just mark the theft of my identity—it ignited a transformation, forcing me to strip away everything that wasn't truly me and rebuild from the ashes.

It turns out, losing myself was the gateway to discovering who I was meant to be.

About Monique

For over twenty years, Monique Lam has been dedicated to driving success in leadership, business development, branding, operations, and sales. She has a proven track record of managing large-scale projects within global organizations and creating marketing strategies that drive growth for small to medium-sized businesses. Monique has collaborated with leading technology brands and entrepreneurs worldwide to build solid marketing foundations and achieve sustainable growth through tailored, insight-driven strategies. Her work guides entrepreneurs and organizations toward success through an adaptable culture of innovation, empathy, and purpose-driven leadership.

As the founder and CEO of the Monique Lam Group, Monique combines her corporate and entrepreneurial expertise to bridge the gap between marketing objectives, sales targets, and overarching business goals. Her unique ability to connect deeply with clients allows her to formulate solutions that drive both business performance and personal transformation.

Monique's background is grounded in a strong academic foundation. She is a certified digital marketing professional and holds an advanced diploma of marketing with distinction, as well as a bachelor of criminology and criminal justice with academic excellence. Her induction into the Golden Key International Honor Society highlights her commitment to continuous learning and staying at the forefront of industry trends.

Throughout her career, Monique's bold yet compassionate approach has driven growth for technology companies and helped countless individuals—managers, peers, and support teams—rediscover their value, embrace their strengths, and lead with conviction. Whether through her consultancy, writing, or workshops, she inspires others to lead with courage and authenticity, achieving personal and professional goals, from job promotions to improved business performance.

Beyond her professional achievements, Monique is dedicated to making a positive impact. She enjoys exploring new cultures, spending time with her family, and giving back to her community. Her life's mission is to help others find their voice, step into their power, and create a life of purpose and impact.

Learn more at www.moniquelam.com.

CHAPTER 15

THE POWER OF COLLISION

*Embracing Disruption as the Spark
for Innovation and Growth*

By Sanj Singh

Did you know that the most brilliant forces in the universe are born from a sudden clash of gas and dust, smashing together under massive pressure?

If you watched it happen, it might look violent. It might seem messy and chaotic. Yet from that unexpected collision, a star is born.

Collisions are messy, disruptive, and sometimes uncomfortable, but they're also the birthplace of creation. The sparks that fly when ideas collide often lead to breakthroughs, innovations, and new ways of thinking, working, and being.

We are taught to avoid collisions, and that's good advice when we're learning to drive or running a marathon.

But what if there are times and places in which a collision is not a catastrophe to bypass, but rather a point of convergence to seek?

Not a disaster to avoid but a clash of circumstances to lean into?

What if the means to success isn't to *run* from collisions but rather actively, consistently and intentionally *create* them?

Over my career I've come to understand the power of collisions—not just of gas and dust in the cosmos, but of ideas and perspectives, in the workplace and in life. It's in these moments of impact that magic happens. Whether it's the intersection of different fields of expertise or the blending of diverse experiences, the result is often a breakthrough; a beautiful fusion that no one could have achieved alone or expected; an alchemy that transforms challenges into solutions, and obstacles into opportunities. We don't need all the traffic lights to be green before we leave home, we just need to begin the journey. After all, 80% of success is showing up.

I've learned how these moments of unforeseen friction, when embraced, can become the driving force behind innovation, progress, and personal growth.

COLLISION 1: NEED AND SOLUTION

"I'm pregnant."

I tried to process my girlfriend's words. I was just nineteen years old and in my second year of college. She was 18. I excelled in high school, winning awards in academics, sports and music and had been offered a football scholarship to attend this university. I come from a family of physicians so as you can imagine, expectations were high. I had already rocked the boat by studying finance, rather than medicine, and by dating a white girl, so news of a pregnancy was a major shock to the system.

Her mother set up a meeting with a priest who suggested that she put the baby up for adoption. My girlfriend refused and at that moment, my life completely changed. It was the first collision— she and the unborn child needed me, and I would have to throw out the script I'd been working from and start a new story from scratch. We felt like we were jumping off a cliff and building the plane on the way down.

I'd be lying if I said my gut reaction was joy. It was panic. Luckily, the solid foundation that had been formed throughout my childhood came through. I was born in India to a very abundant and accomplished family. My mother's oldest brother was Air Mashall of the Indian Air Force. Her youngest brother was second in command of the Indian Army. Another was a radiologist and my mom herself was an ob-gyn. My father was a psychiatrist.

There was an expectation deeply ingrained in me that I should live a life of service.

When I found out my girlfriend was pregnant, I had to reframe what I saw as possible. I made up my mind to act in service to the people who needed me most.

We've now been married for thirty-eight years, raised three daughters and one son and have three grandchildren. On top of that, I have enjoyed a fulfilling career in business, experiencing great successes, a few failures and always finding ways to add value.

What started out as a chaotic and unexpected collision, became the seed of a loving family and a thriving, purposeful life.

Today I am co-founder of several companies and growing a company that uses technology to advocate for women's health. If you had told me twenty-five years ago, I would be doing this work, I wouldn't have believed you. Luckily, I've learned that the most extraordinary things come not from avoiding the unexpected, but from connecting dots, listening to needs and adding value wherever we can.

It turns out, I followed in my family's footsteps of being in service after all. I just did it in my own way.

COLLISION 2: OPPORTUNITY AND ACTION

Years ago I was invited to give a keynote address to over five hundred students at an Industry-University dinner. The challenge was, I was asked to do it just a few hours before it was set to start! I'd just landed late the night before and was jet-lagged when I got the call. The scheduled speaker who was fighting cancer had taken a turn for the worse and I was asked to step in. I empathized with their predicament and agreed. I chose to speak about the importance of embracing stress, since that was authentically what I was feeling!

Armed with just a few words scribbled on a sticky note, I began my talk with, "Imagine you're nineteen, final exams are around the corner and your girlfriend calls…"

After the speech, one audience member approached me and with tears in his eyes said, "I needed that. I've had a rough year, a divorce, the death of a child, and poor grades. I even contemplated suicide. Your talk gave me hope." In that moment, I realized my purpose was to look for opportunities to add value every day to a person, cause or organization. Once I set my mind to that, the opportunities to do so seemed to surround me at every turn.

In 1992 my brother was just coming out of a surgical residency when he reached out to me for help. He had accepted a position in another part of the country and was overwhelmed. He needed help setting up a mortgage, securing the proper insurance and a host of other administrative tasks that came along with a sudden relocation and starting a new medical practice.

I asked him how many of his colleagues found themselves with a similar need to which he replied, "All of them!"

Here was a collision—a problem and an opportunity to solve it. Together we set up a national company to assist physicians through relocation transitions. Innovation can come from anywhere at any time.

My most lucrative business ventures have stemmed from a conversation with someone else. Had I not been curious when speaking to my brother, I wouldn't have learned about the challenges physicians were facing with relocation.

The good news is this is a strategy that is free and available to anyone. You simply have to perk your ears up and listen.

Innovation is not limited to labs and think tanks—it can happen in everyday conversations like it did with me and my brother. It also happened to Sergey Brin and Larry Page. What started as a casual discussion about improving how information was organized on the internet evolved into a multi-billion-dollar enterprise that revolutionized the world. Their curiosity and conversation set the stage for one of the most successful tech ventures in history— you know it as Google.

It's likely that every day, you are presented with a potential business. Pay close attention to your conversations. How many times does a friend say, "I just wish that...," or, "I hate it when..."

Their wishes and complaints are a clue to what the market wants. When you decide to listen, grant wishes and solve complaints, you are standing at the precipice of innovation.

My company, Temple Therapeutics, has been built not just on data, but on stories. Our mission is to redefine what's possible by pioneering a new era in precision medicine for women's health, a market that has long been underserved, dismissed and under invested. I saw those facts as opportunities to fill that gap.

However, we couldn't do that without talking to women!

When we were seeking funding, our banker and I reached out to more than 350 investors and not one of them agreed to fund us. Luckily, I remembered a meeting from years prior that taught me a valuable lesson. I had met the founder of Genzyme, Sherry Sheridan, who had started a company with a mission to treat a rare disease affecting children. No one wanted to fund the research. Year after year, he was told no until one day he set up a meeting with investors and brought with him a mother and her ten-year-old child who was suffering from the disease.

"This," he said, pointing to the family, "is who you're saying no to."

I learned that behind every disease is a human being, an actual life in need of change. As our company grows, that sticks with me. I began to ask the women we served if they would be willing to do video interviews. I knew that if an investor or policy maker could look into the eyes of a woman suffering, they would be less likely to close their wallets and walk away. Stories connect and move people to action.

By learning and sharing our patients' stories, we've been able to show funding sources that their partnership with us is more than an investment—it is a chance to be a part of a historic shift in healthcare and act as a catalyst for changing a woman's life. This led to what will be one of the largest financings completed in women's health.

In every conversation there's an opportunity to add value. It might be a kind word, a well-timed piece of advice, or, on some occasions, the seed of a business venture. The key is to always be listening, stay open to new perspectives and welcome a collision when it comes your way. Lastly, add value to a network before you ask something of them. It goes a long way.

COLLISION 3: VISION AND VALUES

My mom passed in February of 2023. Before she died, I asked her what inspired her to go into medicine. She told me that when she was six years old, and her father was stationed at a British military post in India, her brother had an unknown illness, and it was clearly a life-or-death situation. My grandfather rushed him to a medical office where a physician saved his life. From that moment on, my mother knew she wanted to save lives. Helping others live became the cornerstone of her value system and she lived her whole life in service. That commitment to service shaped my DNA.

My journey into the biotech industry was unexpected but deeply personal. My brother, a urologist, would often share stories of women suffering from interstitial cystitis—women who were mistreated, dismissed and neglected even as their symptoms caused their lives to unravel.

My daughters all worked in healthcare as well, and I saw firsthand the unfair treatment they experienced being women in a male-dominated environment. Our journey wasn't initially focused on women's health, but the data—and more importantly, the stories of the women we listened to—guided us to a mission we couldn't ignore.

I was shocked to learn that endometriosis affects more than two hundred million women and yet it is underdiagnosed and very few therapeutic options exist to treat it or even diagnose it. As I studied further, I was outraged that in the twenty-first century it was still taboo to discuss menstruation and related pain, with some archaic belief systems still associating menstrual pain with signs of witchcraft! This has caused millions of women to suffer silently.

That's not all. As we expanded our interests and decided to launch a sports medicine company recently, I found through initiating conversations that most people did not consider orthopedics to be a part of women's health.

I was dumbfounded! Do women not have bones too? Do they not play sports? Are they not active?

To some it might have seemed like we were fighting a losing battle, but I saw it differently. I know that when vision, values and frustration collide, it's not disruption but a breeding ground for progress.

These moments create the friction necessary to move the needle. For leaders, this is where curiosity becomes a powerful tool. By seeking to understand the values and visions of others, leaders can harness that diversity to create a dynamic path forward—one that respects individual needs and contributions while driving *collective* success.

One of the greatest leadership skills we can develop is the relinquishment of our own ideas. We must be willing to entertain the fact that our idea is but one. The most innovative products and services are created at the intersection of multiple ideas that are then tested again and again until a point of convergence is identified.

I encourage every team I work with to combine, create and converge. Combine perspectives, create ideas that are aligned with collective values and converge multiple visions into a singular vision.

It is from that fusion that the future is born.

COLLISION—COLLABORATION AND COURAGE

Back in my MBA days I was lucky enough to learn from a leadership professor named Ron Edmonds, who marched alongside Dr. Martin Luther King. He taught the importance of knowing which ropes to jump and which to skip—meaning, knowing what to focus on and what to let go. He also emphasized the importance of a shared vision, common values and modeling the way.

When faced with any ethical or moral dilemma, he broke them down into three questions:

1. Is it life-threatening or harmful?

2. Is it illegal?

3. What would your mother say if it appeared in the news the next day?

Since then, I've added a fourth question to the mix:

4. Will this add value to someone's life?

The values we embrace define how we live our lives. The kindness I witnessed as a child motivated me to pursue my purpose. At Temple, we're not just about developing new treatments; we are about challenging the status quo, breaking down barriers and paving the way for others to make an impact.

As philosopher Jose Ortega y Gasset beautifully wrote, "Life is a series of collisions with the future; it is not the sum of what we have been, but what we yearn to be."

Through listening and engaging, we can spark conversations, create massive change, and seek out collisions of needs, values and solutions to ultimately redefine what's possible!

I'm no philosopher, but I often recall a conversation I had with my father right before he died that became a kind of mantra for me, and one I often repeat to my students, family, and friends: "Enjoy the journey, embrace the possibilities."

After all, when joy and possibility collide, success is never too far behind.

About Sanj

Sanj Singh brings over twenty years of leadership experience in biotech and life sciences, with a mission to add value to individuals, organizations, and causes. As cofounder and CEO of Temple Therapeutics, established in 2015, he has positioned the company as a leader in global women's health, advancing it to a clinical-stage and soon to be commercial biotech firm with a robust pipeline. He also co-founded Temple ORTHOBiologics, a sports medicine company recognized for its innovative, game-changing technologies that push the boundaries of healthcare.

Singh's notable achievements include securing strategic commercial partnerships, developing groundbreaking intellectual property, and building a highly differentiated product portfolio. Under his leadership, his companies have raised over seventy million dollars to support late-stage clinical development, secure supply chain agreements, and expand their impact. His influence extends across 14 countries, working with leading researchers and institutions worldwide.

In addition to his entrepreneurial success, Singh serves on the board of directors for BioteCanada, the nation's leading biotech voice. He has also served as Vice Chair of BioteCanada's Emerging Companies Advisory Board. Singh cofounded The Office of Health Innovation and Economic Development (OHI), a nonprofit organization focused on advancing product innovation and healthcare delivery models.

A sought-after speaker and advisor, Singh regularly consults with governments, NGOs, and businesses. He also hosts the podcast ReThink, where he interviews researchers, innovators, and clinicians who are reshaping the future of healthcare.

Earlier in his career, Singh was a professor of entrepreneurship and technology management at the University of Saskatchewan, where he revamped the MBA Biotechnology Management program and led the Wilson Center for Entrepreneurial Excellence as its inaugural director. His leadership earned the center recognition at the Global Consortium of Entrepreneurship Centers conference in Houston, Texas.

Singh holds undergraduate degrees in Finance, Marketing, and International Business, as well as an MBA from the University of Saskatchewan Edwards School of Business. Married for thirty-six years, he has three daughters, one son, and three grandchildren. A multi-sport athlete, he enjoys tennis, football, kayaking, hiking, and mentoring young entrepreneurs, while staying active to keep up with his grandchildren.

Reach Sanj here:

https://www.linkedin.com/in/sanj-singh-64300a6

email: info@templerx.com or info@templeorthobio.com

CHAPTER 16

LEARN DIFFERENTLY

By Tao Zhang

"**W**hat a waste of time."

I shifted uncomfortably in my seat as we waited for the stage lights to turn on.

"Why do we have to be here?"

My mood was about as enthusiastic as a man about to walk the plank. I was inwardly groaning, convinced I was about to trade two precious days of my life for nothing. My wife's cousin Jean had invited us to this same event a few months ago, and we had felt obligated to accept. While it hadn't been one of those over-hyped events full of forced positivity, it hadn't impressed me either.

Here we were, six months later about to see the same speakers, my mind already counting down the minutes until I could escape. As a successful executive and consulting firm owner, I'd been all over the world and heard the most sought-after speakers. My contact list was a who's who of important people and my resume would impress just about anybody. So why did I have to sit through this again?

As one speaker named Sophia took to the stage, the audience, smaller this time, welcomed her with a polite round of applause and I settled in for what I hoped would be a quick and painless event.

I was prepared to be bored. I was prepared to be unimpressed. Instead, I was totally humbled.

I had walked in thinking I knew everything. I walked out wondering if I knew anything at all.

MY WAKE-UP CALL

I was born in a small city in China in the '70s. No one was terribly rich or terribly poor and most worked for a state-owned enterprise. My father, on the other hand, wanted something different and became one of the first solo entrepreneurs in our region. Against all odds, he left a comfortable corporate position and built a successful business in the construction industry. He had no schooling or architect experience but set his mind to connecting with people who did and learning everything he could.

When it was time for me to choose a profession, I decided to become an engineer.

I was an avid gamer, put together my first PC myself in 1997 and it was through gaming that I learned to read and speak English. That skill allowed me to secure a high-profile job in the IT industry as a specialist for IBM and a liaison between Shenzhen and English-speaking partners around the globe. Eventually, I came to the United States and received a job offer in a leadership position even though I was only in my early twenties.

I found myself at a young age being involved in high-profile, multimillion-dollar projects with executives who had thirty years more experience than I did. As the project succeeded and my reputation grew, so did my ego.

So, in 2015, when my wife and I sat in the audience for a second time to hear the speaker, I was not there to learn from the session, but to endure it and if I'm honest, critique it.

Instead, I was blown away. Her tone, body language, and confidence were totally transformed. The message of the session was delivered in powerful stories that captivated my attention. I found myself asking questions, chatting with other audience members and eager to make new connections.

That's when it hit me.

In six months, this person had learned something that caused a drastic change in her public speaking abilities. She knew something I didn't—and it bothered me!

I was humbled, but more than that, I was awake. I didn't know everything after all.

I realized in that moment that for true leaders, school is always in session. The most successful people are willing to put down their egos and *learn*.

The zeros in my bank account and my frequent flier miles meant nothing if I had stopped growing as a person.

I became a student again, an explorer of human behavior and potential, and in doing so, the next step of my journey was revealed to me.

To Expand Your Mind, You Have to Lose It First

I didn't sleep much that night. My mind was buzzing with a new awareness, and I spent hours sifting through my experiences and connecting dots. For years I had been laser focused on climbing the corporate ladder, stayed in five-star hotels and rubbed elbows with the most well-known people in the tech industry. Here I was, in my early thirties already at the top of my career. What now?

What do you do when you've already hit every goal you set for yourself?

You *learn*.

I decided it was time for a new journey. I became an earnest student of philosophy and psychology, poured over the work and research of people like Chris Voss and Carl Rogers and finally understood how learning and listening were the most vital skillsets in communication. Not only that, but they were skills anyone could learn.

I had heard the stereotypes. Heck, I had *been* the stereotype. There was a pervasive assumption that IT nerds were terrible communicators, best left to do their work behind the computer. These days, it's not just techies that struggle to communicate effectively, it's most of us.

Technology has connected the entire world digitally while at the same time leaving us woefully *dis*connected from each other.

We rant, comment, get offended, and are quick to post our opinions but what we don't do enough of is listen and learn.

I decided to be a force for good in helping people learn and started an organization called APEX LEARN. Our mission is to inspire a passion for adult learning, empowering people to grow as individuals and seek opportunities to expand their minds as a bridge to expanding their experience of life!

It's a win-win for me, as research shows that the best way to learn is to teach. By teaching people how to learn and listen, I become a better listener myself. My world has evolved since my commitment to banishing my ego to the back and looking away from what I already knew. We can become so attached to the knowledge we've already acquired that we fail to notice the potential for learning *more*. Our minds contract to fit around our current knowledge base until we commit to our own expansion.

That's the secret not just to success in business, but to fulfilling relationships and dynamic lives of curiosity and wonder. Forget everything you know long enough to make space for what you *don't*.

And when people say you are out of your mind take it as a compliment. It takes years if not a lifetime to master it!

THE LOST ART OF LISTENING

There is a backward hierarchy for success that encourages us to focus on tools and techniques first, and then methodology and principles.

Methodology and principles should come first. It feels counterintuitive in a competitive world, but companies are now hiring talent based on soft skills, and not enough applicants have them! In fact, a LinkedIn report from 2023 highlighted that 92 percent of hiring managers consider soft skills as important or *more* important than hard skills.

The reason most people haven't mastered soft skills is because we call them "soft," and "soft" carries an undeserved connotation of "less valuable."

Empathy, listening, emotional intelligence and communication are not soft skills, they are *core* skills, and without them the interpersonal relationships that are vital to success will suffer and eventually die out.

Still not convinced?

Richard Branson dropped out of school at sixteen, but his creativity and people skills helped him build a global empire.

Steve Jobs dropped out of college and had very little technical training but his ability to inspire people, along with visionary leadership skills revolutionized the world!

Core skills are a lost art and reclaiming them is the secret to strategic success. Here are what I call the "core four."

CURIOSITY

Samuel Johnson wrote that "curiosity is one of the most permanent and certain characteristics of a vigorous intellect."

Even Einstein said he didn't have any special talents but was passionately curious.

Curiosity is one of the cornerstones of success. The more curious you are about other people, their values, their desires and their experience of the world, the more likely you are to be able to provide value, find common ground and expand your own understanding of any situation.

For every negotiation, business or personal, there are an endless number of perspectives, and curiosity is the roadmap that helps you navigate the terrain of biases, subtle nuances and even fear so that you can zero in on a solution.

There is a pervasive belief that we demonstrate intelligence by expounding on subjects we are well versed in when actually we demonstrate intelligence by asking questions.

Our level of intellect is undoubtedly tied to our willingness to admit we know nothing and to seek further understanding.

OPTIMISM

Contrary to popular belief, we are not born as either positive or negative people and even life circumstances cannot dictate our disposition. Optimism is a skill set that can be learned.

If you're put in an environment with four or five other people who are optimistic, you can get curious about why they are, and what possible outcomes they see that you don't. You can also shift your belief around uncertainty. A lot of people we work with at Apex Learn find uncertainty to be a very uncomfortable place and a lack of clarity often leads to a negative outlook.

But as Rainer Marie Rilke wrote, we must try to "love the questions themselves, like locked rooms and like books that are now written in a very foreign tongue." Optimism comes from viewing uncertainty as a gift of discovery.

After all, when nothing is certain, anything is possible!

REFLECTION

We are living in a world of emojis and abbreviations. Spend ten minutes on social media, and you might feel like you are trying to decipher a new language. We have become a society of shortcuts and have moved away from the power of the written word. Writing, however, is one of the best mediums for reflection. Writing forces us to slow our thinking and examine our emotions. In reading what we've written, we can identify patterns, connect dots and gather insights into some of our most complicated problems.

The practice of writing was valued by some of the greatest thinkers of our time. The Roman philosopher Seneca used writing to refine his Stoic principles, and Marcus Aurelius, the Roman Emperor, kept a journal that became *Meditations*, a profound collection of personal reflections that continues to inspire readers to this day.

Writing creates a stream of consciousness in which judgment and filters are removed, allowing for the purest thoughts to come through—our ideas, desires and our truth!

EMPATHY

There is perhaps no greater *core* skill than that of empathy. Whether it's in a diverse workplace or the comfort of your living room, empathy allows you to understand the feelings of others, a quality that is essential for establishing trust and forging strong connections. When another person feels your genuine interest and concern, they're more likely to be honest and generous in their communication. That of course opens the door for you to learn more and give back.

By appreciating and understanding different perspectives, we can respond thoughtfully and make decisions that consider the well-being of everyone involved. Empathy is the bridge that connects you to other people. Their can be no leadership, no teamwork, no successful relationship without it.

BUT HOW DO YOU DO IT?

Typically, when a new member joins us, they're at a crossroads. It's time for a career change, or they have a growing desire to live with purpose and intention. The hard part isn't knowing that they want something but figuring out what that something *is*!

Luckily, we have a proven system to help them.

To truly understand what drives someone, we first help them clarify their top five values. Often we mistakenly believe our values are of equal importance. We experience tension when decisions force us to prioritize one value over another. Not everything is equally important, and in any given pair of values, one will always take precedence. Identifying your top value with crystal clarity is essential.

Next, we invite our members to consider what keeps them up at night—what are the obstacles and sources of misery that you face? These challenges are often directly tied to your values, as they challenge or threaten them. By pinpointing the one or two things that truly disturb your peace, you become more motivated to create change.

Then, it's about leveraging your strengths. Everyone has strengths and weaknesses, and it's crucial to connect your strengths to the problems you want to solve. Core values are what make your strengths effective here. If you rely too heavily on hard skills without aligning them with your core values, success will feel empty.

Finally, reflecting on what worked and what didn't is vital. When we analyze outcomes, we often find ourselves more sensitive to emotions than reasonable in our judgments, especially when working with someone we care about. It's easy to let feelings take over and sideline logical thinking. That's why it's important to take a step back, reflect carefully, and make adjustments as needed. This way, you can really understand what happened and move forward in a more effective way.

Change Is a Choice

If a techie like me—a high-flying guru engineer who once thought he knew everything—can transform into an empathetic, curious, and eager learner, then anyone can. I changed my entire life by embracing the art of active listening, empathy, and a relentless commitment to growth. The key is to keep expanding your mind, infusing your work with passion and love, and in doing so, discover your true self.

As you collaborate with others, not only will you create soul-stirring masterpieces that align with your purpose, but you'll contribute to building a better society. My personal and professional journeys have taken me all over the world. Yet, it was my journey from knowledge to *wisdom* that opened a new world for me.

Imagine that life is a game. Every moment we can choose to be a character in that game whose movements and decisions are at the mercy of a controller, or we can become the controller, building worlds and wielding power. The best-case scenario, however, is when the character and the controller collide into a single being.

It's only in taking the game controller and becoming the driver of our own destiny that we can hear the calling that is uniquely meant for us. We can jump levels and enter new worlds. We can look for sources of power and respawn again and again as wiser versions of ourselves.

In that moment of courageous synchronicity, you are both the artist and the player. You are the writer and the book.

And you can both create the game and *win* it!

About Tao

Since 2018, Tao Zhang has immersed himself in the fields of psychology and philosophy, exploring ideas that have profoundly reshaped his understanding of the world and himself. His journey began in a small city in central China, where he grew up in a loving family. Over time he realized that his parents had sacrificed their own happiness to ensure his, a debt of gratitude he continues to carry deeply.

In his youth Tao faced a pivotal decision: to follow the traditional vocational path or to pursue a high school education with the hope of attending college—a path no one in his family had previously taken. Despite being the lowest-ranked student in his class, his determination earned him a place in the best high school in the area, laying the groundwork for his future achievements.

Tao approached life with the same passion he brought to sports and gaming, whether on the streets, in digital worlds, or in college dorms. His aptitude for gaming translated into a talent for test preparation, enabling him to pass prestigious IT certifications that opened doors to significant projects across Asia. One such project, a large-scale SAP implementation, eventually brought him to the United States, where he became the youngest partner in his mentor's firm.

By the early 2010s, Tao had reached the pinnacle of his career, achieving financial success beyond his expectations. However, this accomplishment left him with an unsettling realization—he had peaked in his thirties. Seeking new challenges and a renewed sense of purpose, he turned his attention to startups, investing his time and resources into ventures that were radically different from the Fortune 500 clients he had previously worked with. The financial setbacks he encountered were less troubling than the question that preoccupied him: Were they truly learning from their failures?

This question led Tao to dive deeply into the platform economy, an area in which he has been actively engaged since 2014. Through his work with Apex Learn, he has crystallized his mission to help adults learn First Principle Thinking in innovative ways, leveraging platform-based environments to create meaningful and lasting change.

CHAPTER 17

THE PSYCHOLOGY OF CHANGE

How to Lead, Influence, and Inspire Growth

By Renata Reid

"A house is made with walls and beams; a home is built with love and dreams."
—RALPH WALDO EMERSON

A sk anyone about their house, and they'll likely start with the style or the year it was built.

"It's a six-thousand-square-foot mid-century modern."

Or perhaps they'll describe it by its features.

"It's a seven-bedroom, four-bath."

What I have learned over the years, however, is that a home is not just four walls, three bedrooms, and one front door.

A house is three thousand memories, eighteen first days of school, and twenty-two Christmas mornings.

Your living room stores the memory of the first time your child walked. Your backyard conjures up the smell of hot dogs cooking on the grill the last time all the kids were home for the summer.

Our homes are alive.

For me, my home was a family member.

You see, my father built my house before moving out of town. I lived there with my kids and their father. The walls held everything from my father's scent to my kids' laughter. I was attached to that house and reluctant to let it go even when life called me to do so. I fully understand the power of sentimentality.

As a Realtor and senior vice president of sales at Sotheby's International Realty Canada, I have learned that underneath every contract, between all the dotted lines, hidden under all the dollars and cents is the thing that truly drives every decision we make: emotions.

THE SECRET TO SALES

I have a secret for selling homes, but it's not my fancy photos and videos or my modern software that seals the deal. What I've learned over a two-decades-long career is that the most important thing I can do for my clients is to guide them, empathetically, through the psychology of change. And I do that through stories. If I can help my clients honor the story that was, while envisioning the story still to come, change is a beautiful process.

If you've ever had to make a big decision—sell your home, get married, end a marriage or make a large purchase—then you know that the most important elements of that situation are hardly ever transactional.

Your palms are sweating. Your mind is running a script of every possible reason it might be a mistake. A cocktail blend of fear and nostalgia threatens to kill the whole deal.

That's where I come in—to act as the bridge between necessary progress and the unmistakable pull of familiarity. That's how all growth happens, right? There is a moment of friction in which what was can no longer be, but what will be is not yet defined. It's in that moment that change is both inevitable and scary.

I started out in interior design, which is a business based on a desire for change. Even though my clients came to me because they were actively seeking change, success depended upon a clear definition of it. I developed a questionnaire to help them get clear on what they wanted to change and why. Eventually, I chose to work in real estate exclusively because I saw how I could help people facilitate transition in a positive way and create amazing experiences for them that had them leaping towards change, rather than being dragged through it kicking and screaming.

What I'm about to share with you are the secrets to guiding anyone through any change with strategic empathy. Whether it's a change in a business model, an employment contract, a relationship or a house, the principles are the same. And understanding them can make all the difference in the world.

Leveraging the psychology of change is crucial for any leader because change triggers resistance and fear. It doesn't even have to be an important change. Ever tried sleeping on the other side of the bed? Or switching up where everyone sits at dinner? Those are totally insignificant things and yet totally uncomfortable. Negotiations in real estate or any business almost always involve asking someone to alter their position, perspective, or behavior, and human psychology naturally resists that.

So how do you lead them to the other side of progress?

While it might be tempting to pull out the data and evidence, the most effective starting point is more subtle; something you can't even see.

Energy.

THE FIRST PHASE OF CHANGE: ACKNOWLEDGING ATTACHMENT

It's no coincidence that when we're speaking about a monumental event, good or bad, we tend to talk about location.

"Where were you when the Twin Towers fell?"

"Where were you when you found out we were on lockdown from COVID-19?"

"I still remember exactly where I was when I heard the news."

The perception is that selling a house is a set of step-by-step logistics. Post a listing, take pictures, schedule visits and collect leads. Yet it must begin on an energetic level.

Psychologists suggest that we lock in a memory by linking it to a *place*. It's called *episodic memory formation*.

If we expand the conversation around this, we can easily see how attachment of any kind can sabotage progress. We may resist moving offices, or become attached to an unhealthy relationship, or stubbornly adhere to an outdated business model simply because it's what we know and have always done.

The first step in any change is precontemplation. There's a problem and we know there's a problem and yet we are reluctant to fix it!

Humans are hardwired to resist change and will do anything to avoid a disruption of their comfort zones. A skilled negotiator who understands this can manage this resistance by acknowledging the discomfort and creating a safe emotional space for change to occur.

This is true for any kind of change. If you're not ready to lose weight, you won't get to the gym. If you're not ready to kick an addiction, you won't seek help. And if someone is attached to their home and reluctant to give it up, it will not sell.

In any negotiation, attachment is stagnation.

A while back a wealthy client came to me whose home had been on the market for years. She needed to sell, and she was frustrated and in tears. I went to her home and immediately saw the problem. Every inch of wall space was covered in expensive art. In fact, the art collection was worth more than the house! It was clear that a lot of other agents felt that the pricey collection might pique the interest of buyers, but I could see what was happening under the surface. My client was emotionally attached to every piece, and what it meant, and where she and her husband had bought them. Her energy was linked to every square inch of wall space in that house.

I told her I understood that this was hard for her. I asked her where all her beautiful art was going to go when the house was sold. She had no answer. I realized that the thought of having to clear these walls was overwhelming to her and I encouraged her to get excited about having art in her new home and to have an estate sale; to lovingly pack up each piece, remember its origin and pass it to someone who will love it as much as she did. Once that was done, her house, which had been on the market for four years, sold within two months.

Sometimes people just want to be heard and understood.

People are more likely to be influenced by someone they perceive as empathetic and on their side.

By recognizing the emotional barriers to change, you can craft a more compelling case for action that feels less like a threat and more like an opportunity for growth.

THE SECOND PHASE: WEIGHING THE PROS AND CONS

The estate spanned an impressive thirty-three thousand square feet and was nestled next to a pristine park. It had belonged to William Stewart Herron, father of Alberta's petroleum industry and was of major historical significance in the Calgary area. Every surface gleamed and the price was right. Yet, it wasn't selling. When I got the call, I visited the house and was immediately captivated by the history. That's when I realized what was going wrong.

The current owner, deeply attached to the history of the home, was subconsciously blocking its sale. He resented that other agents were touting the updated fixtures and the modern touches when the house was screaming to be recognized for its rich and dynamic story.

He had been weighing the pros and cons, which is phase two of any change.

It was clear to me that I would have to reframe the benefits of selling for him and list the home in a way that *supported* his attachment, before I could break it. This is where stories come in.

Story is the cornerstone of any successful negotiation. The person on the other side of the table is attached to a perspective, and it's our job to reframe the benefits of changing that perspective. We can do that with story.

Stories have always served as a tool for teaching, preserving history, and connecting us to one another. Stories engage our emotions and imagination and create meaning by linking events into a narrative we can all relate to. I congratulated him on the care he had taken of the beautiful home and encouraged him to make that same mark on the next place he purchased.

We decided to hold a huge open house and focus the entire day on the history of the estate. Instead of pointing out updated fixtures, we told stories of lavish parties from the past and the first owner's philanthropic initiatives that helped form the community. Soon, guests started sharing their own stories of admiring the estate as children. The current owner was moved by the excitement of the visitors and finally felt confident that his home would be in good hands with someone else. Within just a few days the home sold—and *over* listing price.

THE THIRD PHASE: CRAFTING THE VISION

It's always easier to leave where you are when you know where you're going.

I have found that real estate negotiation and any negotiation for that matter, is often a conversation around identity. An address is not just a street name, it's inextricably tied to our perception of ourselves. Our address ties us to a community, a demographic and a set of experiences. It anchors us to a place in time and is the backdrop for our life stories. Location becomes an orienting narrative so when we move, it's not just a change of scenery, but a transformation of self; a new chapter that challenges the status quo and pulls us into a uncharted territory.

This is true anytime change is present. In every conversation, it helps to understand that the other side is anchored in a three-part vision—a vision that holds a picture of how they see themselves, what they want and how they think what they want will make them *feel.*

At this point, I always invite my clients to sit in the seat of power. Rather than telling them all the reasons they should sell, I invite them to tell me all the reasons they're reluctant to. Then, I ask them what would make them excited to sell so that they start sharing their vision of an even better reality.

This usually results in them painting a beautiful and vivid picture of the future they're dreaming about and allows me to affirm it back to them. I once had a family moving across the country who were devastated to leave their home, and their resistance was blocking offers. I invited the parents and children to walk room by room and share their memories with me. I asked the kids what color they would paint their new rooms, and told the parents how exciting it must be to get to design another home for their family. Soon they were brimming with new ideas and making big plans for their new space. Once they were excited about what the next chapter might hold, I could not only move forward with the listing, but I could present any possible roadblocks without sending them into a panic. With an exciting vision in their minds, a roadblock such as a roof issue that might block inspection is now just a minor problem to be solved on their way to their bright new future.

Whether your conversation is with an executive who is reluctant to change a policy or a child refusing to go to school, guiding the other party toward a vision that's even better than their current reality is ultimately the key to success.

THE STRATEGY THAT NEVER FAILS

You might notice that the one quality present through every single phase of change is empathy.

My mom and dad, Lucy and Steve Ozdoba, are my biggest inspiration, having emigrated from Poland to give our family a better life. Their strong work ethic and commitment to being of service has always inspired me to do the same in giving back and caring for others around me.

The empathy that was instilled in me by my parents informs every interaction I have with the families I work with.

Human beings are in a unique and sometimes frustrating loop of both wanting change and being naturally wired to resist it. It is only through empathy that we can balance our instinct, which is to cling, with our desire, which is to grow.

My sales record is consistent. My quota is always surpassed. Yet what I am most proud of is that I love what I do, and I do it in service. Commissions are nice, and indeed necessary, but my true motivation is to leave every client better than I found them; to guide them from fear to hope and hold their hand through the choppy waters of change so they can move forward into a new and brilliant future.

That's the goal of any negotiation, isn't it? To inspire others to relinquish their hold on the past and present and step into the future with trust, hope and excitement.

We can view change as a scary unwelcome enemy. Or, we can view it as a trusted guide—one that reminds us that we are alive, shakes us out of complacency and leads us exactly where we are meant to go.

About Renata

Step into the world of luxury real estate with Renata Reid, a distinguished name in Calgary's property scene. As Realtor and Senior Vice President of Sales at Sotheby's International Realty Canada, Renata feels it is an honor and privilege to serve her clients, bringing unparalleled expertise, integrity and innovation to all her clients whether they are buying or selling their dream homes.

Her extensive experience and impressive track record make her the go-to realtor for those seeking exceptional service, a twist of fun and remarkable results. Renata hosts grand open houses that create an immersive experience showcasing her listings as homes rather than mere properties. She meticulously curates each event, filling the space with inviting decor, soft lighting, and carefully chosen live music to create a warm ambiance. By featuring local gourmet treats and engaging activities, she encourages potential buyers to envision their lives within the walls, from hosting gatherings to enjoying quiet evenings. Renata's attention to detail and ability to evoke a sense of belonging not only captivates visitors but also helps them connect emotionally with the home, making her open houses memorable and effective.

Renata is not just a highly sought-after Realtor; she is also a compassionate philanthropist dedicated to making a difference in her community. Her commitment to various charitable causes is matched only by her dedication to her family. As a loving mother of two amazing kids, Renata cherishes her large extended family, balancing her career with a rich, fulfilling personal life of fitness, adventure and travel. Her circle of friends and family is a testament to her warm and engaging personality, reflecting the genuine connections she fosters in every aspect of her life.

Community building is at the heart of Renata's mission. She is an active and beloved figure in Calgary, known for her efforts to strengthen local networks and support neighborhood initiatives. Whether through hosting events, volunteering, or simply lending a helping hand, Renata is a driving force behind Calgary's vibrant community spirit.

And let's not forget her loyal canine companion! A passionate dog lover and owner, Renata finds joy in the simple pleasures of life, often sharing her love for dogs with her community.

Ready to embark on a real estate journey with a leader who combines expertise with genuine care? Contact Renata Reid today. Whether you're buying, selling, or seeking insight into Calgary's dynamic market, Renata is your ideal partner.

Experience firsthand why working with Renata Reid is not just a transaction but a transformative journey toward your real estate dreams.

Let's make magic happen together!

To contact Renata, email her at renata@renatareid.com or visit her website at www.renatareid.com.

CHAPTER 18

BREAKING THE CYCLE

The Healing Power of Strategic Connection

By Laura Engel

The hair on the back of my neck stood on end, and bile rose in my throat.

My father had abruptly turned the car onto an old dirt farming road, slammed on the brakes, and ordered my mother to get out.

My two sisters and I were ten, twelve, and sixteen, and we sat paralyzed in the all-too-familiar sickening silence that hung in the air anytime we found ourselves in the terror of the unknown.

We had been driving home from a religious convention and were having a good time, laughing and talking about the weekend and the friends we had seen. None of us had noticed my father's mood darkening. As soon as we were far enough away that no one could see, he ordered my mother to get out of the car, raised a gun to her head, and said, "If you don't start including me in your conversations, and stop making me feel left out, I will blow your head off in front of the girls!" Without another word, they both got back into the car.

For the remainder of our two-hour drive home, the four of us delivered an Oscar worthy performance of a happy family whose sole focus was to delight and entertain the monster who held our lives hostage.

THE POWER OF ACKNOWLEDGMENT

Sadly, the event I just described was not an isolated incident. My identity was shaped in a house of shadows where darkness, fear, and secrecy dominated, and explosive conflict ruled; a place in which even a minor misstep could lead to a violent outburst. Staying alive depended on my ability to adapt on the fly, correctly read any given situation, spot danger before it spotted me, and trust only myself for survival.

Even as a child, I could see the pattern that provoked the rage. My father wanted to feel seen and heard, and I knew that my life depended on making that happen. If I didn't, he'd make himself seen and heard in terrifying ways. Now, as an adult and educator, I have learned that when someone is acting out, what they are seeking is acknowledgement. They want to know, and feel, that they matter; that their presence is desired, that their absence would be felt and that their feelings are worthy of respect.

I know now, of course, that we can all learn to tune into the needs of others and have powerful conversations that cultivate connection.

I don't know if I could have helped my family *then*, but I know I can help other families now, and it's my life's work to do so.

As a child, I was overwhelmed by the lack of control I felt and the environment that in no way aligned with my personality. I was required to navigate situations far beyond my emotional capabilities. As an educator, I've observed the fact that our school system may not be abusive, but it does cultivate the same sense of misalignment, especially for children under five. I can personally attest to the fact that when a teacher engages the tools necessary to help their students feel seen and heard, then offer personally tested and successful suggestions to their administrative staff, they are shut down and instructed to use the outdated methods approved by people who have not taught in a classroom for years or ever.

Most school systems do not provide the space, fresh air,

curriculum, or adult understanding necessary for a child's developmental needs. These children are often confined to rigid structures that stifle their natural need for movement, autonomy, exploration, and play.

The result? Children who are frustrated and stressed, and teachers and parents who are out of patience. Just as I had witnessed my father lashing out when he felt unheard and unseen, children express their discontent through dysregulated behavior, which is often labeled and misunderstood rather than addressed with empathy and strategic connections.

The key to resolving this lies in creating an environment that fosters clear and empathetic communication. I could tell that was never going to happen in the traditional school setting and I couldn't stand back and watch the same distress I'd seen play out in my home repeat itself in the classroom. I decided to build a forest school, Little Forest Explorers, and base it on the needs of the developing child as proven through the latest scientific research on brain development. The school is in a 100 percent outdoor setting, and free from the constraints of a disconnected administration. I was finally free to use my strategic conversations with both the children and their parents and the results surpassed my expectations.

Why is this important? Because if you can learn how to speak to children you can speak to anyone. After all, most of us look like adults, but we're still operating from behind the lens of a wounded inner child.

If you learn to speak to a child, you are by default, learning to influence an adult…

THE TOOLS OF CHANGE

All our lives we are thrust into negotiation environments we don't choose. It might be a hostile coworker who suddenly shows up at your desk. Or an aggressive partner who reveals a side of themselves you never saw coming. You might find yourself in an argument with a loved one or a debate with a police officer who pulls you over for speeding. There will always be situations we find ourselves in that require us to adapt. The tension, fear, and uncertainty are palpable, and we, as the negotiators, must work within these constraints to achieve a safe and positive outcome.

If you have tools at your disposal, you're in a much better position to come to a collaborative solution.

About a year ago I came across Chris Voss' book *Never Split the Difference* and realized that the conflict and communication strategies I had been using since I was a child had names—mirroring, labeling, and tactical empathy. Recognizing the effectiveness of these tools in early childhood development, I began to implement other lessons from Chris at the school.

A calculated question helps me to guide the conversation in a specific direction without triggering defensiveness. When a child demands something of me that I cannot produce such as to make it stop raining, I ask, "How am I supposed to do that?" This question often brings up giggles and inventive ideas on how to make these impossible requests possible.

Bending reality is employed to teach children the "if this, then that" theory: "If you do this to Johnny, how do you think he will respond?"

"Getting to no" helps me view some children's reactions in a different light. The "No!" response during challenging moments allows me to see these instances not as obstacles, but as opportunities to come to a better understanding of what matters most to them to generate a deeper connection.

Every conversation centering around self-regulation with a child is a negotiation. The same is true in every conversation with an adult. You might be talking about contracts and facts but underneath it all, each side has an emotional goal. Emotion is always in the driver's seat. How we handle a conversation ultimately determines whether it escalates or deescalates. This is where successful communication comes into play: it's the ability to clearly convey ideas while understanding and addressing the emotions and needs of all parties involved. By recognizing emotional drivers, acknowledging fears, and using strategic tools like tactical empathy, calibrated questions, and nonverbal cues, we create a foundation for authentic connection.

When we master this, we wield the most powerful tool of all—effective communication that transforms conflict into growth.

EMPATHY IN ACTION

One of my favorite examples of strategic communication comes from one of my two-year old students. Run primarily from the emotional part of her brain, Sofia would break down into tears and tantrums when she was not able to communicate her feelings fast enough. Using consistent strategic conversations, Sofia was able to practice engaging the more rational part of her brain as an immediate reflex.

As Little Forest Explorers, we spend a large part of our morning exploring our surroundings. Sofia was a very slow hiker as she was fascinated by all that nature had to offer. Every piece of sour grass growing was a temptation to indulge in. Every leaf needed to be studied, and every flower smelled. Though this is the curiosity that is fostered in our school, Sofia was often met with an encouraging, "Come on, Sofia. Let's keep moving." When she made it clear that she was not ready to continue, either through a defiant, "No!" or just ignoring the teacher's persuasive attempts, a strategy needed to be employed. We needed to keep on schedule, while supporting Sofia's curiosity. I got down to her level and looked at what she was examining. Taking a genuine interest in her discovery, I asked, "What did you find?"

Sofia: "Rolly-Polly."

Me: "A Rolly-Polly?" (Mirroring to let her know she was heard)

Sofia: "Uh-huh." (Pointing to show me where the Rolly-Polly was)

Me: "Would you like to look for more Rolly-Pollies?" (Calibrated question getting her to think about the prospect of more discovery)

Sofia: "Yes!"

Me: "How do you think we can do that?" (Another calibrated question giving her control of an outcome I am looking for)

Sofia: "Go." (Pointing to her moving class)

Although still slow-going, we were indeed moving. This strategic conversation, although basic and simple, ended with the result that I needed— to keep Sofia close with her classmates and teachers, while still feeling content that she was gaining something instead of losing something.

We had been implementing these strategic conversations over the course of the year, and when Sofia was almost three an exchange occurred that showcased the benefits of strategic conversations. Sofia was yet again lagging behind on our hike when another teacher, using an impatient tone called out, "Come on, Sofia, catch up!" Sophia stopped what she was doing and said, "I'm feeling overwhelmed. I hear, Sofia, Sofia, and I don't know what to think. You need to speak to me kindly so I can understand you!" I was moved to tears, witnessing Sophia's remarkable growth in self-regulation and clear expression. Sofia was not only taking charge of her reaction with clear and precise language, but she identified her emotion (feeling overwhelmed) and gave a solution to solve her feelings (speak to me kindly). Now, imagine if these strategic conversations continued through the first five years of her most active brain development, how self-regulated, emotionally articulate, and grounded she can become as she continues to mature.

It's not too late. As adults, we can practice this kind of self-awareness and emotional intelligence and bring those attributes to every conversation we enter. Imagine how much progress we'd make and how much change could be enacted if we saw each other not as adversaries but as containers that hold deep and dynamic emotions. Before we handle facts, before we discuss data, we've got to learn to attend to emotions.

Emotions, more than anything, are what drives the direction and speed of our goals.

The Mirror Effect

It's the oldest debate in the book...bedtime! Negotiating with a four-year-old is tough, but trying to show a parent how their actions impact their child? Now that's a challenge of Olympic proportions! One parent, frustrated with bedtime routines, expressed confusion about their child's behavior:

"Liam acts like he's lost his mind! I tell him to get ready, and he just starts screaming. I don't know where he's getting this behavior from—certainly not from home."

He didn't realize the irony. After all, this parent admitted, "Sure, I raise my voice sometimes, but I'm the parent. He shouldn't be copying that!"

This points to a fundamental truth about human behavior: we are wired to mirror each other.

Children reflect what they see in their caregivers, not just in body language, but in tone, energy, and emotion. It's a natural response—humans seek resonance with those around them, often unconsciously. When a parent gets frustrated and raises their voice, the child learns to respond in the same way. This isn't about defiance or disrespect; it's about matching the energy they're receiving.

The same is true in adult interactions. When we engage with others, they don't just pick up on our words—they mirror our tone, volume, and emotions. If we bring frustration or anxiety into a conversation, the other person is likely to reflect that back, escalating tensions. Conversely, if we approach with calm and patience, it encourages the same in return.

We are built to match those around us, which means we have the opportunity to set the tone. The key is recognizing the power we hold in how we present ourselves—because others, including our children, are paying attention and mirroring back what they see.

DRIVING CHANGE

Imagine a world where children, before the age of five, have already mastered the art of self-regulation and critical thinking. This critical window of brain development is a once-in-a-lifetime opportunity to lay the foundation for lifelong skills. By focusing on self-regulation early, we can foster a generation that thrives in handling stress, decision-making, and emotional intelligence as adults. The ripple effects of this could be monumental—adults who approach challenges calmly, think deeply about problems, and lead with empathy rather than impulse.

So, what if you started today? What if you tried using some of the strategic conversations this chapter has suggested with your child and with the adults in your life? The future is shaped by the actions we take *now*. If we can raise a generation of self-regulated, critically thinking adults by starting today with intentional conversations, the world will be a better place.

And if we can remember that in each of us lives an inner child longing for this type of connection, the possibilities for growth and success are endless.

It's too late for me and my dad, he passed away several years ago. I don't excuse his behavior but, now as a professional, I understand it.

We are all born pure and hopeful, and if my work can preserve that for a child and evolve a parent, I've done my job in this world. Remember, people will forget what you said, but they will never forget how you made them feel.

I hope I make them feel seen, that I make them feel heard, and that through me they see that they are important, worthy, and that the world is a brighter place because they are here.

About Laura

Laura Engel is an early childhood educator who has worn many vocational hats before finding her true calling in teaching. Laura received her degrees in Early Childhood Education and Child and Adolescent Development. Laura has an educational career spanning fifteen years, bringing a wealth of experience and a vibrant sense of humor to her work. Believing that the traditional educational system has lost touch with the individuality of children, Laura advocates for a learning approach that prioritizes the unique pace and curiosity of each child. Instead of focusing on the rigid timelines and milestones often imposed on young learners, she favors instead a philosophy that allows children the freedom to simply be children. True to her adventurous spirit, Laura created a 100 percent outdoor learning environment where children are free to explore, play, and learn in nature's classroom.

The driving force behind Laura's teaching career stems from growing up in an abusive household where she felt trapped, unseen, and unheard, shaping her passion for creating a different path for the children she teaches. Determined that every child in her class feels seen and heard, she approaches each day with the purposeful intention of ensuring her students know they matter—because, in her world, everyone deserves a standing ovation, even if it's just for peeling their own banana.

When she's not guiding her young explorers, Laura can be found traveling the world, collecting experiences and adventures that fuel her own love of discovery—something she's determined to pass on to her students. With kindness at the core of her teaching and a belief in expecting the best, Laura Engel continues to inspire both children and adults alike.

The wisdom of these strategic conversations has transformed countless lives. Imagine the impact that can come from equipping caregivers with the tools to raise emotionally intelligent, self-regulated children who will be our next generation of decision-making adults. By amplifying this message, you can help shape a future where young minds thrive in environments of empathy and critical thinking. Anyone interested in collaborating to strategically expand this mission is welcome to reach out to Laura by visiting littleforestexplorers.com.

CHAPTER 19

MAKE IT HAPPEN

By Charlie Pesti

"The art of communication is the language of leadership."
—JAMES HUMES, AUTHOR, SPEECHWRITER

My story is a direct reflection of the importance of understanding that communication is a deep, multi-layered vehicle for failure, success, struggles, triumph, change, and growth.

It's my story as a Hungarian entrepreneur who dropped out of college and spoke no English yet went on to create and run a successful communications business in the United States.

It took guts. It took perseverance. Mostly, it took a commitment to understanding the universal principle upon which effective communication is built: desire.

THE BUSINESS MIND EMERGES

I was just eighteen years old when I was drafted into the Hungarian army. The base, filled with able-bodied youngsters, had limited access to the things that brought us joy—coffee, tea, soda, and snacks. It might not sound like a big deal, but something as simple as morning coffee provided some comfort and familiarity in the absence of family, and we all missed it. I realized there was a market here and a potential business opportunity.

I had a friend at home who owned a retail store that sold all the things we couldn't get on base. I struck a deal with him and began to smuggle coffee, tea, soda and snacks to the base on weekends. This was strictly forbidden, and I was taking a huge risk, but the business skyrocketed. My first shipment sold out in two hours. I became the "go-to" guy for tuck!

One Sunday the commanding officer on duty asked to see me. My heart raced as I walked to his office. I was sure my purposely not-classified military secret (I needed paying customers) had been found out.

"We have a problem," he said, in a stern and intimidating voice—just as you would expect from a commanding officer. "You are not allowed to do any commercial activities on the base."

"I know," I said, and looked into his eyes, searching for answers about my fate.

"That is not the biggest problem, however," he said. "The more pressing problem is, your shop is out of Coke."

He gave me a six-hour pass to leave the base and replenish my soda supply and told me if it happened again, I would be on prison food for the remainder of my time there.

So, I guess you could say my first successful business was an illegal snacks, coffee and soda shop, but it taught me an important lesson.

People's needs and desires are at the heart of every successful venture. The commanding officer didn't want to shut me down. He just wanted me to continue to create value and stay attuned to the needs and preferences of people on the base.

That's when it all clicked. People precede profit. If you can understand people, the value you create for them will generate profit and you will always reap the benefits of success.

THE SECRET TO COMMUNICATING WITHOUT WORDS

I grew up in a very small town in Hungary and after my stint in the army, I decided to open the first pizzeria in our region. I had no money to invest, but I knew there was an opportunity there, and I was confident I could make it work. I had a German friend with a wealthy grandma, and she was as close as I was going to get to securing an investor.

Although I loved to cook, I had no prior experience managing a restaurant and spoke only a few words of German—and she didn't speak any Hungarian. How could I convince this accomplished woman to trust us with her money if we didn't even speak the same language? I needed to sell my idea to her in a way that she would understand.

So I went with my gut, sold my heart out and hoped for the best.

I knew nothing about the art of negotiation, but I was honest, had passion and heart, and that day I learned that negotiations are, for the most part, a transfer of emotion. I believe that although she couldn't understand every word I was saying, she could feel my passion for the project, and it was enough to convince her to write a check.

In retrospect, it could have been that a grandma was the best investor for a pizzeria—who better understands how food can bring people, families and communities together? Or perhaps I reminded her of her own grandchildren and their desire to succeed. Whatever it was, it amounted to my second successful business venture, the first pizzeria in a small Hungarian town.

CONNECTING THE DOTS

The pizzeria flourished and went on to be acquired by my retailer friend, the same one who was my supplier on the base. Sometimes all you have to do is connect the dots and see who within your network could be a valuable partner.

For my next endeavor, I went to work for a trucking company. This was a time in my life when I wanted to settle down, mitigate risk, and take a break from the financial volatility that came with the ups and downs of entrepreneurial pursuits. Back in the good ole' days, driving a truck across continental Europe paid very well. And for the most part, I was paid in stable western European currencies. By this time, I spoke German very well and was often asked to stop driving the truck and help in the office instead. These project-like assignments made me realize that speaking different languages was a significant strength and could be a stepping stone to a more lucrative career.

As a truck driver, I made great money, but there was a ceiling on the income and no ladders to climb. As an administrative executive, however, I could expand my reach, define my career graph, build my network and secure business connections that were higher up the ladder of success. I recognized that in knowing how to speak German, my world could extend far beyond Hungary.

That got me thinking about what I needed to do next.

Shakespeare said, "It's not in the stars to hold our destiny but in ourselves."

In my case, it was a bit of both. One day, as I was coming into work, I noticed a new sign on the window next to ours: Schedule Your English Lesson Today!

An English teacher had opened a business right next to us. I thought, "If I could master the art of nonverbal communication *and* learn the most widely spoken language in the world, I could provide value in virtually any room I walked into."

I walked into her office and signed up. Next, I walked into my boss's office and negotiated a deal: he would cover the cost and benefit from the result of me speaking another language. What I didn't know then was how these actions would change the trajectory of the rest of my life.

If You Want to Keep Succeeding, First Understand the Problems!

Fast-forward to twelve years later. I applied for a job to establish a business in a new country. The job attracted me for two reasons: It required both my entrepreneurial mind and communication skill set. Side note: I couldn't have even toyed with the idea of working with a foreign company if I hadn't spoken three languages.

After passing the first round of the application process, the hiring managers asked me to prepare a presentation about myself. This approach allowed them to compare applicants on paper, advance a few to a shortlist, and eventually pick who seemed to fit the best based on corporate criteria—education, budget, experience.

They wanted to see how I could sell *myself*, gauge if I could sell their products and compare me to other applicants. But I didn't want to compete with anyone on paper. Instead, I wanted to show how I could create value for their business.

I came prepared. Not by their standards, as I came with only two slides. Slide number one had my name on it. Slide number two had all the logos of companies I was already connected with and did business with in the past. Those logos happened to be potential customers for this company.

For me the interview started when I entered the room and was instructed to wait a few minutes. I used that time to pick up on the dynamics in the room and observe body language to learn as much about them as possible.

Our brain is hardwired to equate power with the amount of space people take up.

Body language provides an amazing amount of information on what other people are thinking and who the key decision makers are. In fact, research conducted at UCLA has indicated that only 7 percent of communication is based on the actual words we use. The remaining 93 percent is split between 38 percent tone of voice and 55 percent body language.

Since I now knew who the decision maker was,, I started copying his body language. I even picked up on the speed and the accent he spoke with, and used this information to connect with him. When I started explaining how I knew the businesses on slide 2, what I did for them, and how I was connected, he leaned against the wall and started mirroring *my* body language. It's something we all do unconsciously when we feel a bond with the other person.

He started asking great questions. He was relaxed and engaged, and I knew, I had him. The conversation had no resemblance to a job interview anymore, because it wasn't. It was now a business negotiation.

They hired me on the spot and at a higher salary than they had originally budgeted for. I didn't bring them a resume, I brought them customers. I brought them value. I knew that what they ultimately desired wasn't for me to perform on paper, but to bring business, and I could do that for them on day one.

One of the most critical aspects of any negotiation is to understand the negotiating partner's perspective and figure out what they really want and need. Seldom are these things on display—they exist between the lines or in the fine print.

If I had followed their instructions and prepared a presentation about myself, I probably would have lost. On paper I was not the perfect candidate. I had no college degree, never worked for well-known corporations, and my pay expectations were high. I had to rely instead on my ability to listen to, read, and understand people.

People, in any room, at any level, want to be heard, helped and most importantly, *understood*.

HOW TO LISTEN AND BE HEARD

Today, I am the owner of a successful full-service B2B PR and Marketing agency. I am based in the United States, but work with a fully remote, international team, with colleagues in the US, India, South Africa and multiple countries in Europe. Businesses from all over the world come to our agency with vastly different needs and wants. I would wager that we secure more long-term clients due to our willingness to listen more, understand better, and speak less. Much less.

We do not conform to the corporate constructs and have done away with the "cc" culture. Every team member is accountable for their own work, and you can be sure the work doesn't stop when the time is up, but when the work is done. Not everything is always smooth sailing, but when a project does go awry, we listen, pivot and know exactly how to get it back on track.

One day I got a phone call, and as soon as I picked up the phone, I could tell by the tone of voice that something was wrong. It was one of our clients, the CEO of a large company, and he wasn't happy. When he had hired our PR firm a few weeks prior, he shared that his company's goal was to increase brand recognition. Within a few days we had secured him an interview with a leading media outlet in his industry. The journalist had written a balanced, full-page editorial article that positioned his company as one of the go-to solutions in the market.

When I asked why he was upset, he said, "It has been two days, and we haven't received any new leads from the article."

Now it made sense.

Although he had asked us for "increased brand recognition"— an external verification that the company is worth a look, a call, a meeting—what he actually wanted were qualified sales leads.

This made me realize two things: (1) that despite the in-depth sales interview process we take clients through, we had to be better in managing expectations, and (2) our onboarding process needed to be restructured to include deeper questions that distilled our clients' goal down to the exact result they wanted.

Now, when a client shares their goals, we know to paraphrase their words back to them.

"It sounds like you ultimately want x. We'd love to build a comprehensive plan to get that result. Would you be open to us doing abc?"

Statements and questions like this give the client a chance to clarify their meaning and give us a chance to ask questions that lead to alignment and results.

THE THREAD THAT CONNECTS US ALL

Plato wrote that human behavior flows from three main sources: desire, emotion and knowledge. Plato was born around 427 BC, and yet his words still ring true today.

Successful communication, personal and professional,

transcends the written and spoken word and instead relies on our willingness to understand the emotions and desires of others as a means of creating value and growing our own knowledge.

These universal values connect us all and have for centuries. From a soldier smuggling sodas to create value, to a young entrepreneur using nothing but passion to secure an investor, to a seasoned business leader understanding the deeper needs of clients and partners—every experience taught me that true communication lies in understanding human desire. It is in silent exchanges, unvoiced needs, and shared understanding that we find our greatest power and our most effective strategies. To succeed in life, business, and relationships, one must learn not just to speak or to hear, but to listen, feel, and connect on a level where words are helpful, but not necessary.

The road to success is never a straight line, but it is a road that is always paved with the learnable qualities that connect us all. Master the art of connection and communication, and you will always be able to change the world.

Words are powerful. They can build bridges and inspire positive change, or they can cause pain and destruction. It is my mission to always do my part to make the world a better place and use communication as a catalyst for growth. It is my genuine request that you strive to do the same.

About Charlie

Charlie Pesti is a prominent figure in the global supply chain and logistics industry, recognized as a leading PR and marketing strategist for nearly a decade. As the founder and chief make-it-happen officer of his namesake agency, Charlie has cultivated a diverse team of professionals from around the globe, dedicated to addressing comprehensive marketing, PR, and consulting needs of businesses.

Charlie's journey began nineteen years ago. His career has seen a remarkable upward trajectory, encompassing various roles that range from operations to sales and business development. These experiences have provided him with a deep understanding of industry intricacies, ultimately inspiring him to establish his own agency in 2018. Throughout his career Charlie has collaborated with organizations of all sizes— from startups to Fortune 100 enterprises—on the client side while also engaging with leading business and trade media on the service side. His exceptional rapport with journalists, combined with a bespoke approach to each client, has enabled his team to deliver unparalleled value in navigating the complexities of the B2B ecosystem.

Beyond his professional accomplishments, Charlie has led a multifaceted life. His diverse experiences include serving in the Hungarian army and founding the first-ever pizzeria in his hometown at age nineteen. He speaks three languages and has lived in three countries on two continents.

In addition to his professional pursuits, Charlie is an avid cook and motorbiker—two passions that reflect his passionate and adventurous spirit. His unique blend of experiences across cultures, countries, continents, and expertise not only enriches his work but also drives his commitment to making a meaningful impact in the world of business.

With a keen eye for innovation and a dedication to excellence, Charlie continues to shape the future of PR and marketing, ensuring that his clients thrive in an ever-evolving business landscape.

Learn more:

https://www.pesti.io

https://www.linkedin.com/in/charlie-pesti-6088718

CHAPTER 20

MY WAY: NEGOTIATION AND QUALITY, NOT DEBATE

By Camilo R. Gomez

I t was the early 1990s, and we were on the brink of something monumental.

Every day, the air buzzed with the excitement that comes with innovation and unprecedented progress. At the academic stroke institute I directed, our neurovascular team had engaged in a breakthrough collaboration with our interventional cardiologists, adapting their endovascular techniques to the diagnosis, prevention, and treatment of stroke. At a time when similar work had been largely restricted to radiology practitioners, we were poised to introduce a unique clinical perspective, one destined to forever change the way stroke patients were treated, an evolution so profound it would launch an entirely new medical subspecialty called *interventional neurology.*

Our vision was for interventional neurologists to have the opportunity to directly treat complex stroke victims using minimally invasive techniques, expediting their care and without the need for major surgical procedures. Such an approach promised to consistently allow patients to recover faster, while reducing the risks of traditional neurovascular surgery.

Lives would be saved, and futures once marred by disability could be reclaimed. We were standing on the threshold of innovation when the platform was suddenly pulled out from under us. In our school of medicine, the position of chair of radiology had been vacant for several years, and our new dean had finally found a candidate. Unfortunately, her candidate viewed our neurology-cardiology interventional collaboration politically and operationally unacceptable. Thus, he delivered an ultimatum—him, or us. If he was to accept the position, we had to cease and desist all our work immediately!

We had no choice but to comply. Years of dedication were crushed in an instant. I was devastated, not just for myself and our team, but for the patients who I knew we could help. In light of the void left within my academic, clinical, and personal priorities, I decided to resign my tenured position and find a way to fulfill what I believed to be my professional destiny.

It turned out that I was right. Today, interventional neurology is an accredited medical subspecialty, and I've had the honor to be one of the first certified operators, as well as the founding chair of the national certification committee.

I had been "right" in my vision. I had been "right" in my initiative. Yet having been "right" had done nothing to help my cause at the university because "right" isn't what moves the needle. I can't help but wonder how my situation may have turned out had I been familiar with negotiation tactics and had used them to influence our new dean, or even her candidate for radiology chair. Would he have eased his opposition to our efforts in developing this medical discipline? Perhaps even aided our efforts? If I had known how to apply *active listening, tactical empathy,* and such, would the value of our work have been better communicated?

As I have reflected on these doubts, one question has always weighed on my mind: Had I mastered the art of *strategic conversation,* would more stroke lives have been saved?

A BRUTAL WAKE-UP CALL

"You owe us two million dollars in payroll taxes."

Suddenly the air was sucked out of the room and, even though the IRS agent was still talking, I wasn't hearing her. I heard only one thing—*two million dollars!*

At the time, I was running a successful medical practice, and I had entrusted the financial operations of our firm to a close family member. Until that moment, I had been confident of his abilities. But in that instant, arguably one of the most sickening moments of my life, such confidence was suddenly wiped out, and replaced by disbelief, disappointment, and anguish.

While consumed by a mélange of anger, betrayal and self-loathing, I began taking steps to remedy the calamity I faced. As the CEO of the company, I was personally responsible for the economic restitution of the funds owed, comprising unpaid payroll taxes plus accrued interests and penalties. The aftermath? It would be another decade before I could say that I was finally coming out on the other side of such a mission. And yet, I had no one to blame but myself. As a former US Army officer, I knew all too well that leaders are ultimately responsible for the actions of his team members. The burden of command...

My family's financial well-being had been compromised right under my nose. I hadn't been paying enough attention. I had failed to have vitally important conversations. Retrospectively, there had been a trail of breadcrumbs I should have recognized. I would ask questions, receive vague answers, and I would fall short by not asking for clarification.

Had I taken the time to sit and *actively listen*, I would have noticed the irregularities and the lack of eye contact. I would have identified the non-verbal tale-telling cues of deception. Such a discovery could have easily been followed by using *tactical empathy, labels, mirrors,* and *calibrated questions* to uncover the hidden information that was driving the damaging behavior.

The experience became an excruciating lesson on the importance of attention, awareness and persistent curiosity.

You don't understand the jargon? *Mirror...*

You aren't sure of the other party's true wishes or intentions? *Label...*

Something doesn't seem right? *Paraphrase...*

The benefit of applying these negotiating tactics to acquire information, instead of asking straight up questions, is the sense of empathy piggy-backed onto them; one that implicitly influences the recipient to comfortably expose the hidden emotions behind their actions. However, it would be some time before I understood the amazing power of approaching difficult interactions from a negotiating vantage point.

ARE YOU IN A NEGOTIATION OR A DEBATE?

Hence, after enduring career hurdles and personal life blunders, how to negotiate my way through future obstacles became a priority for my operational growth.

Four decades of medical practice, including over thirty years as an interventional operator, researcher, and educator, led me to the realization that physicians are not systematically taught how to negotiate, but rather how to *debate*, and there is a vast difference.

I have often been told I am opinionated and a difficult debate opponent. Well, I have certainly had a lot of practice. Academic medicine has taught us all to embrace the intellectual jiujitsu of debating the empirical basis of competing opinions and, just like in martial arts, to walk away victorious by virtue of our informational and confrontational prowess. The skillset required for excelling in debates includes knowledge, expertise, experience, and rhetoric, but not empathy! As a debater our mission is to prevail by applying intellectual brute force, not by a deliberate attempt at influencing the other side to voluntarily agree to our terms or comply with our demands.

Conversely, effective hostage negotiation techniques, as taught by accomplished mentors such as Chris Voss, Derek Gaunt, and Nick Peluso, rely on the establishment of *rapport* for the purpose of influencing a *behavioral change* that results in the outcome we deem most appropriate. Developing rapport requires mastering, among other skills, *active listening* and *Tactical Empathy*, two closely related tactics that allow the negotiator to influence the course of discussions by projecting a sense of safety and focused attention. In turn, the person on the other side of the table finds himself being heard and understood and is more likely to reveal the driving emotions and ideas behind his own demands. Such revelation results in our discovery of pathways leading to optimal resolution and deal-making.

In short, a debate relies on knowledge; it is a competitive exchange of opposing viewpoints, where the goal is to demonstrate the superiority of one's position by undermining the arguments of the opponent. By contrast, in a negotiation the ideal objective is to facilitate a collaborative process that leads to an optimal deal along an ostensibly frictionless exchange. Empathy and rapport, instead of assertion of dominance.

Back in the day, when meeting with our dean, I had possessed all the knowledge I needed to win a debate. I could have made the most solid case for my vision; an impenetrable informational fortress that would overwhelm any discussion. But what I didn't have was the skillset to negotiate and maneuver the conversation to a point at which both her and the aspiring radiology chair candidate would feel understood, in turn opening their minds to the possibility of a deal by eventually declaring: "That's right!" My knowledge of neurovascular advances was useless in the absence of the ability to persuade. I was never going to succeed by merely rattling off facts and data. I needed to project empathy, sensitively inquire, tune in to the wants and fears of the new chair, and present a path that responded to those fears by gently shifting his perspective.

Debate is about evidence and assertiveness; negotiation is about human behavior. One keeps parties on opposite sides of the table, while the other brings them closer as they overlap as components of a collaborative Venn diagram; creating an outcome whose worth is greater than the algebraic sum of the two parties.

As for you, the reader, if you want to be sure if you are debating or negotiating, ask yourself this question: "Am I seeking a practical and empathic solution or just trying to prove my point?"

A BLACK BELT FOR QUALITY

An important consequence of my experiences and realization was that I prioritized learning how to better negotiate, beginning with the recognition that every version of human interaction is a form of negotiation. As physicians, we negotiate with patients, their families, other physicians, different healthcare disciplines and hospital administrators, among others. Since our mission is that of protecting and prolonging human life, influencing all these groups is of paramount importance to our success.

Years later business school opened my eyes to disciplines with which I was not familiar, including *Lean*, *Six Sigma*, *Theory of Constraints*, and yes, *Negotiation*. It also provided me with a working knowledge of accounting, finance, strategy and operations. Armed with this new set of skills, I felt more comfortable discussing both medical and nonmedical issues pertaining to my own practice or to hospital processes.

Emphasizing learned principles during negotiations with hospital administrators, supply chain officers, and even medical staff leaders; shedding light on costly strategic and operational errors in judgment, as well as their impact on quality of care became one of my favorite *leitmotivs* of such interactions. By *actively listening* and using their own information to generate appropriately *calibrated questions*, I found it possible to persuade many a committee that their original conclusions about the topic of discussion needed revision.

I've always had a special place in my heart for quality and its optimization, as it translates to the best value, determined by the ideal cost relative to a superlative outcome. Unfortunately, most medical organizations continue to confuse cost with value and succumb to the obsession of indiscriminately cutting cost, often to the point of compromising value.

In parallel, the medical community has not historically embraced the quality improvement tools celebrated by other sectors of the economy, particularly Lean and Six Sigma. However, experience demonstrates that enhancing medical care quality through error minimization and waste reduction is feasible and meaningful.

In the context of my business education, I became certified in Lean Six Sigma, a discipline that, similarly to martial arts, incorporates "belts" of different colors to identify the level of the practitioner's expertise. I'm proud to have worked my way up to the highest level, and this has made a huge difference in my ability to be an effective consultant. Applying *Tactical Empathy* has led me to better understand how to influence groups to embrace the importance of quality projects, or to *paraphrase* their covert needs, driving them to ultimately agree by stating: *That's it!*

I can confidently assume that the decision makers I'm addressing do not want to waste time or money, so I can ask *calibrated questions,* or use *labels* and *mirrors* that prompt them to reveal their focused desire, so I can tailor my solutions to meet their needs. Mastering the art of *active listening,* using *dynamic silence,* and resisting the urge to argue or overwhelm the conversation with facts and data, creates value and leads to better negotiation outcomes.

PUSHING THE ENVELOPE

A friend once told me that if I ever wrote my memoirs, I should title the publication *Against the Grain.* It is no secret that I have a habit of pushing the envelope, particularly when I am passionate about something, and I make no apologies for such a style.

To illustrate, in the early 1990s I wrote an editorial exhorting the vascular neurology community to embrace the concept of treating stroke as a time-critical emergency. It seemed clear to me that such was the only pathway to finding successful management strategies, considering the rapid rate at which affected brain cells die. I then found myself in a firestorm of acrimonious mail from numerous colleagues and peers. I was bitterly scolded for advocating a rush to stroke care at a time when we "didn't have definitive treatment".

Presently, my essay is still widely quoted, as timely management of stroke is understood to be of vital importance in achieving optimal outcomes. Once again, I was right! However, being right is inconsequential unless the concept becomes applicable to practice. Scientific results cannot translate into saving lives if they live only on paper. It's up to us to take data and theory and persuade human beings of their meaning and worth. Along my career, I've stuck my head out again and again, against the grain if you will, learning each time that being right wasn't enough. Thus, I have focused on consistently applying effective, persuasive communication, particularly as the underpinning of negotiation.

An important attribute of leadership is the courage to be different, provoke change, and argue against the *status quo*. I'm a physician and, as such, a scientist. Nevertheless, I rely heavily on my instinct while engaged in opposing exchanges, and I complement it with techniques learned from mentors and leaders in the field of hostage negotiation. I'm grateful to all of them.

As it turns out, being an effective communicator and negotiator is more than a skill, it's a path to fulfilment. Knowing I can influence others in ways that drive change gives me the confidence I need to keep doing bold things and doing them in my own way. It almost feels like a homage to the late Frank Sinatra and the song he made so popular, whose lyrics amply describe how I have lived my life: my way.

I like to think that because I have done it *my way*, someone's mother, father, or child is alive, that because I have pushed forward, someone out there can wake up today, have dinner with their family, and do the work that they love. Moreover, as I continue to lead by example, it is conceivable that some of my students may also learn to do it *their way*, making the world better and healthier.

About Camilo

Having practiced academic medicine for over forty years, Camilo R. Gomez has been a leader in the fields of vascular, critical care, and interventional neurology. In fact, he has pioneered some of the most successful and innovative approaches to the treatment of stroke, both conceptually and operatively. Along his career, he has mentored countless physicians, as part of their undergraduate and postgraduate educational programs, engendering a legacy of specialists that continue to follow in his footsteps.

As a seasoned educator, he is a skillful lecturer, an accomplished communicator, and a sought-out speaker, one who has engaged audiences both nationally and internationally. His conferences predictably convey critical, insightful, and unique points of view, as he typically challenges the listeners to think "out of the box" and not to simply conform to the *status quo*. His somewhat irreverent and out-of-mainstream style is palpable in the pages of his 2012 book *The Downgrading of American Healthcare*.

With a solid background in business, and as a Lean Six Sigma Black Belt, he excels at evaluating clinical systems operations. His leadership has steered quality improvement teams to achieve significant and measurable successes in process enhancements, earning recognition from prominent healthcare organizations.

Upon witnessing how the landscape of healthcare practice and medical education have changed over the years, he has most recently introduced negotiating concepts borrowed from law enforcement and business as the means to enhance the ability of physicians to effectively influence patients, families, peers, students, and administrators. This refocusing is now incorporated into his never-ending search for improving all outcomes, optimizing not only the health of patients but also the well-being of physicians, aiming at reducing the pervasive and insidious growth of professional burnout, with all its negative consequences.

As a speaker and consultant, he can help organizations identify the root causes of problems in clinical operations, and then craft practical solutions, implement necessary modifications, and ultimately improve their overall performance. In parallel, he can assist them in the development of strategies to systematically negotiate issues relative to conflict resolution while promoting culture optimization.

He enjoys playing chess, badminton, and pickleball, as he also loves spending time with his wife, Kayla, their children and grandchildren.

Learn more:

https://en.wikipedia.org/wiki/Camilo_R._Gomez

https://www.linkedin.com/in/camilo-r-gomez-md-mba-a9837ab

CHAPTER 21

THE POWER OF THE PAUSE

By Bruce Sheridan

The impact came out of nowhere, a brutal, unexpected blow that sent shock waves through my body and a sharp, searing pain through my mouth.

I can still hear the sound of my tooth cracking from the root. My head spun as I spit blood onto the floor, the metallic taste a sickening symbol of what was an all-too-common occurrence at our house. Usually, I knew how to dodge my father's wrath, but that day, I wasn't quick enough. Before I knew it, I was in the car, my hand clamped over my mouth, as my mother, cold and detached, instructed me on the lie I needed to tell the dentist— the story of a bike accident that never happened, and the consequences if I failed to convince him otherwise.

It's no wonder that by the time I was twelve years old, I'd made it a point to figure out which bad seeds in the neighborhood would buy me beer so I could numb out what had become an intolerable existence.

When I got to college, I drank even more but somehow managed to get an engineering degree from Georgia Tech. By the time I was twenty-five, I had a job offer from a top power company in Miami. In no time at all, the president of the company took a liking to my work and promoted me to a leadership position, putting me at a table with people twice my age and years more experience.

As you can imagine, Miami was a breeding ground for trouble for a young guy with a big ego, a big paycheck and a regular habit of substance abuse.

Things were starting to get out of control. I was staying up all night, using cocaine and waking up the next day with no sense of time or responsibility. It was clear that if I didn't get a handle on things I was going to lose my job, end up in jail, or worse, land on the coroner's table.

It was after a particularly rough night of binge drinking and drugs that I ended up where most people like me ended up—on the floor, in a sweat, praying for God to fix my life. At first, nothing happened, and the same resentment toward an absent God that I felt throughout childhood started to creep back in.

About three weeks later I visited a friend on a Saturday morning. When I opened the door, a beautiful girl I had never seen before was standing in his kitchen making breakfast.

My friend sauntered out of his room and with his usual sense of humor said, "Glad you're here. I need your help. This girl won't sleep with me!" When I asked her why, she replied, "Because I'm a Christian."

She looked up from the skillet, "Do you believe in God?" she said, her gaze peering through me. I immediately said yes, but her next question stopped me in my tracks.

"But," she said, her eyes never leaving mine, "do you have a personal relationship with Jesus? And if not, would you like to?"

Then she went quiet, back to frying eggs, seemingly unaware of the flood of thoughts she had unleashed in my head. Everything was in slow motion. How could I have a relationship with someone who is dead? What would Jesus want with a guy like me? It was probably just thirty seconds that passed in silence, but for me it felt like an eternity, and I found myself whispering a convicted, "Yes."

She stopped cooking and asked me to say a prayer with her. What I felt can only be described as an electric current running through me, like a light went on in my heart. The next few weeks unfolded in a blur. I started reading the bible daily and after getting a DUI, decided to attend my first AA meeting.

God had answered my prayer. Four months from that morning

in my friend's apartment, I was back on track at work, sober, going to church and teaching Sunday school.

That girl cooking breakfast gave me two gifts that day. She asked a life-changing question, and she gave me the gift of silence so I could hear the answer from within.

THE REWARD OF REDIRECTION

We often think of listening as something we can only do if someone else is in the room. Listening has become synonymous with hearing what someone else has to say.

Yet if you look up the word *listen* in a thesaurus, the list of synonyms includes words such as "accept," "observe," and "take notice."

Listening extends far beyond conversation. We can listen to the guidance of our inner voice. We can listen for God's answers to our prayers. What I invite you to do as well is to listen to your *circumstances*.

Any time you're at a crossroads, or a change has been thrust upon you, you can complain about it, or you can accept it, observe it and take notice of what this new circumstance might mean for you or the gifts it might hold.

In 1993, I left Miami to become director of quality at a multimillion-dollar company in Charlotte, North Carolina. Then, I pivoted to teaching business systems at Queens University, which led me to start my own consulting business. After four years, GE Capital recruited me and at my wife's urging, I accepted the position.

Later, I moved to Bank of America and spent eleven abundant years there, until the 2008 financial crisis hit. In 2009 the bottom fell out. I lost $600,000 in stock options and had to sell the house, my luxury cars, and our boat, and figure out how to drastically downsize our lifestyle. Hundreds of thousands of people in my field had been laid off, so as you can imagine, navigating the job market was like swimming in an ocean with thousands of hungry sharks. Luckily, PNC bank called and asked me to come on board to help them integrate with National City Bank in Pittsburgh. Over these years and through all this upheaval we were also raising four children!

Eventually, I discovered a company called EOS, which stands for Entrepreneurial Operating System. The concepts they taught to cultivate business growth were the very same concepts I had been using for more than a decade, only they had a streamlined system framing them. I met with the company, felt complete alignment and left that meeting knowing I wanted to start my own franchise. My wife wasn't so sure, but I knew in my heart that it was the right move. There was only one other time I defied my wife, and it was the time I pulled my new Harley Davidson into the driveway. Luckily, she forgave me for both, and since then, my company has thrived tremendously.

I share this with you because each major life shift, brought with it a sacred pause—a moment that felt like panic but was really life redirecting me, pushing me to follow paths I wouldn't have found on my own.

We're so conditioned to react that we often don't take the time to *reflect*. The numerous reinventions I experienced were a gift.

They led me to my purpose, which is to help other people tune in to their dreams and make them a reality.

THE SILENT STRATEGY

Nobody on their death bed ever says, "I wish I'd spent more time working."

And yet most entrepreneurs began with a vision of time freedom only to find out that they're working more hours than before and for less security.

As a Certified EOS® (Entrepreneurial Operating System) Implementer and EOS Worldwide Equity Partner, my job is to help business owners restructure and create resonance as a bridge to profit.

I can't tell you how many business owners have a moment in which everything seems to come to a screeching halt, and they think, "Hang on. This isn't what I signed up for. Where's all the freedom?"

EOS was created from a passion for helping people get what they want out of their businesses and as a result, get what they want out of their lives!

We focus on three things: the company's vision, its traction, and developing a healthy leadership team.

I now guide clients through the entrepreneurial operating system, but anyone can use this. You've just got to learn to tolerate the discomfort of silence.

There's an Indian mystic named Rajneesh who was quoted as saying, "Real creativity can only come out of silence."

Think of yourself like an organization going through a restructuring. You now need to holistically look at your life in the six main categories:

Vision, data, process, traction, issues, and people.

What is the vision of your life? What kind of resources and facts support that vision? How can you make some progress and gain some traction? What are the potential obstacles and who do you have on your side to turn to for support?

Any time I meet a new client, we start with a ninety-minute session to set the vision, and I ask three very important questions:

What makes you jump out of bed and come to work?

What do you want to be the best in the world at?

If we were meeting three years from today, what would need to happen personally and professionally for you to feel like a success?

I ask those questions, and then I shut my mouth!

That's no easy feat for someone like me. I spent years in the corporate world, where we demonstrate our expertise by talking about how much we know. I used to think that if I was quiet, people would assume I didn't know the answers. Later I understood that staying quiet, listening and holding space to allow for ideas to germinate is the mark of an effective leader.

What I learned in my work with my clients is that my silence allows them to think, and to eventually reach the conclusions that are most aligned with their goals.

If I speak, I interrupt that vital creative process and their focus shifts from reflecting on their vision to responding to my words. It sounds so simple, but human beings have a tough time being quiet.

Something happens in our amygdala that causes us to feel like we just may burst if we don't fill the void and speak out! Silence in a negotiation is a surprisingly powerful tool because when you stop talking, you give the other person's brain the space it needs to process information, sort through details, and reach new conclusions. Silence isn't just about pausing; it's about creating a mental environment where deeper thinking can occur.

In my visioning session with clients, we meet in front of a giant white board. We invite everyone present to share their ideas and then one by one, we kill and consolidate, striking and blending ideas until we reach the result that feels right.

Ninety percent of this session is spent in quiet. I must constantly remind myself to refrain from giving any advice that guides them away from their own perspectives and over to mine.

When they do speak, I write, and as we walk back through all the ideas, I mirror back to them what I heard and see if it still matches what they were trying to communicate. After some back and forth, we land on the result!

Try it. Set a meeting with yourself or with a partner to have a visioning session. Sit in front of a whiteboard and ask yourself what you want your life or business to look like in three years. Sit there in silence, no matter how long it takes, until the ideas and answers start to flow.

It's ironic, isn't it? Sometimes strategic conversations are the most powerful and productive when no one is talking at all.

A LIFE WELL LAUNCHED IS A LIFE WELL LIVED

A while back my oldest son had reached that all too common place in adulthood that holds both frustration and endless potential: the crossroads.

He was struggling to figure out what to do with his life. I had been coaching for thirty years at this point, but this moment, more than any other, was a true revelation of my purpose. I sat with him for four hours, guiding him to create a solid vision in four principal categories of life—God, family, career, and budget.

At the end he had not only a vision that inspired him but a road map for making it real! He was so moved by the experience that he suggested I help other young adults through the same process. I could have waved off the compliment and gone on with my day, but instead...

I paused.

I thought about what it might be like to do that, how the work I did with business owners might hold universal principles that a young person could benefit from. I stayed quiet to see what my heart had to say about it.

And in that pause Life Compass Inc. was created. Life Compass is a Christian non-profit through which I help young people discover, plan for and pursue their dreams. It also inspired me to write the book *A Well-Launched Life*, guiding young people to seek resonance as a benchmark of success and create intentional and fulfilling lives.

My roles as a Christian teacher, a coach, an author and a business growth consultant all stand in stark contrast to the twelve-year-old boy drinking beer and getting into street fights *and* to the twenty-five-year-old hot-head addict.

I wonder where I might be had I not leaned into each crossroads of my own; if I hadn't noticed when God had pressed "pause" or bothered to take time to consider the lessons and opportunities in those moments of reckoning.

I know now that life is not a straight line. It's a windy road fraught with detours but if you approach it with humility, curiosity and empathy, you will always be led somewhere better than you were before.

Every day, new clients call my office because they've reached a crossroads and need guidance to navigate it. And every day, I am reminded that my name might be on the door, but the guidance they need is usually already inside them. The light-bulb moments almost always come not when they're listening to *me* talk, but when they are brave enough to be silent so they can hear their creativity speak.

Silence is a lost art form but a lucrative one. I have been lucky enough to build a thriving career doing what I love, and what I know for sure is that success doesn't come from endless conversations about data analysis.

Profit, progress, and purpose are not found in a boardroom or on a spreadsheet.

They are found in the seat of silence, in the space between words, in the power of the pause.

About Bruce

Bruce Sheridan had humble beginnings. Bruce grew up in a lower-middle class Irish Catholic family of eight in Union City, New Jersey, across from midtown Manhattan. An interesting fact is that Union City is the most densely populated city in the US. This overcrowded city was a tough place to grow up.

Attending Georgia Tech, Bruce worked twenty hours a week and earned an engineering degree. While at Georgia Tech, he was a member of the varsity track team. He ran the 110M HH and 400M IH. Bruce left Georgia Tech with $110 in his wallet and began his career as an engineer for Florida Power and Light (FPL) in Miami.

At age twenty-five, he was asked to sit at the table of the Miami division president. Bruce spent seven years under the tutelage of the Union of Japanese Scientists and Engineers. In 1989, FPL became the first non-Japanese company in the world to win the coveted Deming Prize for Quality. Taking advantage of living in Miami, Bruce was invited to be a member of the 1988 USVI Olympic Sailing Team.

Bruce spent five years running his own consulting business to help other companies benefit from his Deming Prize lessons learned. He was recruited by GE to become one of its Six Sigma Master Black Belts. While at GE, Bruce was recruited by Bank of America, where he held several leadership roles over a span of eleven years.

In 2009, the call to be an entrepreneur led Bruce to again launch his own management consulting business. Bruce worked with senior leadership teams helping them improve their businesses. On one assignment, he spent eighteen months in London at Barclays on the Consumer Bank Risk Management Leadership Team.

In 2017, one of Bruce's clients suggested he read *Traction*, by Gino Wickman. He fell in love with the Entrepreneurial Operating System, EOS®. EOS is a simple, proven operating system that helps small businesses focus on priorities and make weekly progress. When a small business needs help in achieving its goals, Bruce knows he can help.

One of Bruce's passions is his 501(c)(3) Christian nonprofit, Life Compass Inc. Life Compass™ is a simple methodology that young adults can use to figure out their purpose and passion and create a plan. In 2022, Bruce wrote an award-winning book, *A Well-Launched Life: How Young People Can Live an Intentional, Fulfilling Life.*

CHAPTER 22

RISING TO THE PEDESTAL

Build Trust, Find the Overlap, Lead with Empathy

By Anis Attarwala

It was the summer of 2009, and I was untouchable.

Every deal was smooth as butter. The commissions were coming in hot, and I was quantum-leaping through every sales goal, smashing my competition and enjoying the perks that came with being number one in the office.

The view from the top was fantastic, so the first deal that fell through barely registered, a small blip on an otherwise smooth day. I shrugged it off, chalking it up to a client's indecision. The second deal, I dismissed as a fluke—a bad week, nothing more. But by the time the nineteenth deal crumbled, I couldn't ignore the truth any longer. It was summer. This was the season we usually crush it. And I was getting destroyed.

The thud of reality hit hard; I'd been knocked off my pedestal. The question now wasn't just *why* I'd fallen—but how in the hell I was going to climb back up.

An Early Lesson in Perseverance

I was born in England, where sports are quite competitive but quite different from American sports. I'd never seen an American football or a baseball. Nonetheless, at eight years old, I joined little league baseball. I was the last one picked and didn't have a single hit all season. I remember thinking, "Next year, I'm going to show these guys!"

223

I practiced every day no matter the weather and watched every game I could. When the next season started, everyone remembered me for striking out at every at-bat. I was picked last again and put at the end of the batting lineup. I could hear my teammates groaning when it was my turn to bat. I got up to the plate, took a deep breath, and hit the ball all the way to the parking lot! The groans turned into cheers! That year, I made the all-star team, and not only did it feel great to have accomplished my goal, but it lit a fire inside me.

I continued to chase new challenges, always striving to beat my personal best and prove to myself (and to any doubters) that I can do anything if I commit to it.

My career in real estate started as one such challenge.

I was looking for a new apartment for myself and called an agent who had just posted an ad for an apartment. When I asked to see it, she said the apartment was rented but that she had something else.

Classic bait and switch.

I couldn't believe the apartment posted five minutes before my call was already rented, but I told her I was willing to see other spaces. I explained to her that space was of the utmost importance. I also told her I'd pay her a full commission if she found the right apartment for me.

The following day I met her to see an apartment, and it was the exact opposite of what I was looking for.

I was angry that she'd wasted my time with one tiny apartment that met none of my criteria, and I let her know how disappointed I was in the level of service she had provided. Needless to say, I moved on.

The following day, I met with another broker, but when we got to the building, he didn't have a key. After an unsuccessful attempt to buzz into the building, he walked all the way back to his office on 78th street, making me wait a full forty minutes. He showed up drenched in sweat, and again the apartment was not at all aligned with the needs I had shared with him. More time wasted.

Later that day while running an errand, I saw a sign that read Agents for Hire. I walked across the street to Manhattan Connection, interviewed on the spot, and was hired. Real estate runs in my family. My mom is in the business as a broker in Princeton, New Jersey. My father built homes in Princeton, and my sister is in commercial finance. I knew I could do this, and I could do it better than the two agents who had given me the runaround!

In my first full month at the agency, my manager, Tal, offered a new plasma TV to the top-producing agent for the month of October. I was determined to win that TV. My parents had one of those old-school TVs from the 1990s, and they deserved an upgrade. He shrugged me off, assuming that as the newest agent I didn't stand a chance.

When the results came in, I beat the person who trained me by five hundred dollars in gross commission to take the number one spot. To this day, my parents still use the TV I won for them.

For the next several months I was number one. No one could beat me.

That's when the bottom fell out. Nineteen failures in a row were a huge blow to both my ego and my bank account. I could no longer call this a stroke of bad luck, and in my head I was back in little league baseball, recalling the feeling of being counted out and the determination to prove myself.

I needed to do something, and *fast*.

I analyzed every aspect of my technique. I unpacked every communication strategy I used with clients, looking for gaps in efficiency and understanding. I documented my processes, assessing the user experience and identifying any area in which I had become complacent. I took radical responsibility for what I did wrong and vowed to not repeat my mistakes. By the last two weeks of August, I was number one again, producing $45,000 in gross commission. I had clawed my way back to the top.

I realized that this hard reset had forced me to build a set of steps. In revisiting core principles of sales and customer service, establishing discipline and documenting procedures and strategies, I had designed a blueprint for becoming the number one producer in the company.

I also realized that these tactics work for virtually any goal. Apply what I'm about to share with you, and you'll find yourself on a pedestal of your own.

You'll also be much likelier to stay there!

BUILD TRUST, NOT RAPPORT

In 2009, I closed 105 deals. I was ahead of the next agent by 65 deals. No one was even close. But when I lost nineteen deals in a row, I *had* to change my philosophy. I stopped working for money and started working for *deals*.

In any negotiation, if you believe that you are the most important part of the equation, deals die.

Many agents believe if they can build rapport through small talk, they'll have an edge. I believe that clients can sense this and are turned off by it.

When I show apartments, I may be a bit aloof until they warm up to me. I do this on purpose to show that I am willing to be patient and earn their trust, unlike every other broker working overtime to force a fake connection. People can feel a lack of authenticity, and if they are discerning enough, contrived camaraderie can kill a deal. I also show clients that I value their time. If I'm showing a client more than one apartment, I'll have an Uber ready to take us to the next stop. This always surprises people, as most NYC agents don't bother to go the extra mile. It's a small investment that's absolutely worth it to me.

It's akin to a server giving you a free dessert. You'll often tip extra because of it! This strategy creates a subliminal obligation on the part of the tenant to pay you back in some form or another, and it has paid dividends for me over the years. The more you invest in clients unexpectedly, the more likely they are to stay loyal and send referrals.

Taking a cab or Uber also sends a message that I am busy and therefore need to be efficient. It shows that I care about their comfort. I'll never be the sweaty broker that makes someone wait forty minutes. Finally, it shows that the small price of the Uber is nothing to me, which creates a perception of success.

When we're in the car, I don't make small talk—I speak mostly about what we saw and what they thought. I am polite and warm, of course, but it's clear that I am focused, and clients appreciate that. I don't need to make friends.

Still not convinced?

Imagine a slick, fast-talking attorney who might impress with charisma and speed, but often misses the nuances that lead to success. In contrast, a lawyer who isn't interested in the spotlight and instead *listens* more than they talk, can craft winning strategies and well-prepared arguments that resonate with judges and juries.

Building trust is more important than building rapport because trust is the cornerstone of sustained relationships, while rapport is often superficial and fleeting. If you want to become the best, you've got to demonstrate expertise, not just a winning personality.

You need feedback, not friendship. And they need results.

Find the Overlap

One of the concepts I've developed over the past fourteen years is called the overlap. The way a deal comes together is if both buyer and seller agree on price and terms. If the buyer doesn't agree to the seller's price or the seller doesn't agree to the buyer's price, there is a gap, and that gap is where deals go to die!

In my experience, there are dealmakers and deal-breakers. Many agents make the mistake of representing only their buyer. I became a dealmaker because I'm committed to finding the overlap, that sweet spot where the buyer inches toward paying a little more and the seller inches toward selling for less so that a buffer zone forms, and a deal gets done.

In negotiations it's vital to create a space where both sides feel heard, valued, and understood—a space where values overlap. This isn't just about finding common ground; it's about making sure everyone feels that their interests matter. When both parties sense that their values are recognized, it's easier to build trust and work toward a mutually beneficial solution.

In negotiation no one ever gets *exactly* what they want, which is why it's essential to create a sense of victory through a values overlap—where each side feels as if they've gained something meaningful, even if it's not everything they initially sought.

This buffer zone is accomplished by understanding what's most important to both sides. The gap may be in price, closing date, renovation, or something else.

This idea of tuning in to where values overlap can be applied to a lot of different scenarios. I happened to learn it through real estate, but it works in any negotiation, personal or professional.

You see, if the agent, or negotiator, is merely a messenger, they have no control. You've got to be willing to lead. The buyer wants to pay a certain price, and the seller wants to sell at a certain price, which leaves a chasm in the deal. Neither side wants to cross the chasm because they feel they are giving something up.

In this scenario, the deal reaches an impasse.

Overlap is designed to eliminate this.

In 2014 I put the concept of overlap to the test in a high-stakes negotiation. An agent hired me to negotiate a $12 million apartment deal, with a target of closing at $11 million. Representing the buyer, we initially planned to offer $10.5 million, but I strategically started at $10 million, which brought a counter of $11.75 million. After several calculated moves, I managed to get the seller down to $11.4 million while keeping the buyer's expectation at $10.75 million.

Knowing the buyer was willing to go up to $10.75 million, I raised our offer to $10.6 million, continuing to narrow the gap.

The opposing broker aimed to stay above $11.2 million, but I used the shrinking overlap to build expectations on both sides. The broker called me and said I could get a deal done at $11 million. I went back to the buyer and told them that I could get a deal done at $11.1 million just in case I needed some space. I asked if they would take the deal if I couldn't get it any lower, and they said yes.

Eventually, the broker offered to close at $11 million, which aligned perfectly with our goal. I had already set the buyer's expectation at $11.1 million, so when we finally settled at $11 million, the buyer was pleased, and the deal closed smoothly. Overlap prevailed, and both sides felt they had won.

The point here is that if I only followed my client's strategy as a messenger, I would never have been able to make a deal in their favor.

Facilitating an overlap, especially when each side isn't fully aware of it, isn't manipulation or dishonesty—it's smart negotiation. It's about guiding both parties toward a solution that satisfies their core interests, ensuring a positive outcome for everyone involved. When your intention is to help each side feel understood and respected, you're not deceiving them; you're creating a win-win scenario where both parties walk away feeling as if they've achieved something valuable.

Overlap works, and every time I forget that fact, I lose.

Empathy Closes Deals

As I look back on that summer of 2009, I realize that being knocked off my pedestal was the best thing that could have happened. It forced me to abandon the comfort of complacency and dig deep into the fundamentals that had brought me success in the first place. I learned that winning isn't about staying on top— it's about constantly refining your craft, building trust, and creating real value in every interaction.

In 2009, after that losing streak, I analyzed my behavior, responses, and actions. I looked at myself from a third-party perspective so I could determine my clients' perspectives during our work together. I retrained myself to lead with empathy and understanding, rather than knowledge and data.

If you're only mastering the technical skills, with your brain focused on the commission, you'll fail. It sounds counterintuitive, but if you want to make a lot of money, you have to forget about the money altogether and focus on the people. Whether you're a lawyer, a doctor, a real estate agent, or a furniture salesman, it's not enough to know your industry. You've got to know your client—what moves them, what scares them, and what they desire most.

The failures that summer were painful, but they were also the catalyst for a new level of discipline, strategy, and resilience. They taught me that the real victory in any negotiation or challenge is not in having things go your way but in facilitating a zone of overlap in which everyone involved feels served and valued.

The fancy awards and big commission checks are just a way to keep score.

About Anis

Anis Attarwala has a proven, long-standing track record of success in the real estate brokerage and property management businesses. His service levels, acumen, and negotiation skills have earned him several Agent of the Year awards, and his client list includes some of the biggest names in real estate worldwide. He has closed thousands of transactions and advises his clients on strategic real estate transactions.

Anis founded Pocketbroker, a New York City-based brokerage and property management company in 2018 with an emphasis on service and technology. His leadership and real estate knowledge have rocketed Pocketbroker to one of the best firms in New York City. He has developed a paradigm for closing real estate transactions that he teaches his agents to find similar success.

Anis's passion for real estate is unparalleled, and his clients gravitate to him because of his knowledge, reliability, and dedication to his clients. Whether he is drawing from his background in economics from the University of Chicago or his transactional experience, his clients trust his advice with major decisions.

As an investor in tech start-ups, Anis has a keen eye for new technologies. He is taking his interest a step further and starting up a software company to make property management companies more efficient.

Too much of his NYC clients' chagrin, Anis is an avid Philadelphia sports fan, poker player, and foodie. He enjoys spending time with his family and playing with his dog.

Connect with Anis:

www.pocketbroker.com

info@pocketbroker.com